SWU-NAP- 027

UNIFORMS OF RUSSIAN ARMY DURING THE NAPOLEONIC WAR VOL.22

UNDER THE REIGN OF ALEXANDER I
EMPEROR OF RUSSIA BETWEEN 1801 AND 1825
THE TEMPORARY FORCES

From the Viskovatov's greatest work:
"Historical description of the clothing and
arms of the Russian Army"

English translation by Mark Conrad

SOLDIERSHOP PUBLISHING

AUTHOR

Aleksandr Vasilevich Viskovatov born 22 April (4 May New Style) 1804, died 27 February (11 March) 1858 in St. Petersburg, Russian military historian. He graduated from the 1st Cadet Corps and served in the artillery, the hydrographic depot of the Naval Ministry, and then in the Department of Military Educational Institutions. He mainly studied historical artifacts and the histories of military units. Viskovatov's greatest work was the Historical Description of the Clothing and Arms of the Russian Army.

ACKNOWLEDGEMENTS

A Special Thanks to NYPL and other institutions for their kindly permission to use some images of his archives, collections or books used in our book.

Title: **UNIFORMS OF RUSSIAN ARMY DURING THE NAPOLEONIC WAR VOL. 22**
The temporary forces By A.V.Viskovatov. Serie edit by Luca S. Cristini. First edition by Soldiershop. August 2018 Cover & Art Design: Luca S. Cristini. Plates re-colorations by Anna Cristini.
ISBN code: 978-88-93273541

Published by Soldiershop publishing, via Orio 35/4 - 24050 Zanica (BG) ITALY. wwwsoldiershop.com

UNIFORMS OF
THE RUSSIAN ARMY
DURING THE
NAPOLEONIC WAR
VOL. 22

UNDER THE REIGN OF ALEXANDER I EMPEROR OF
RUSSIA BETWEEN 1801 AND 1825

*

THE TEMPORARY FORCES

Russland.

1. Husaren-Regiment   2. Husaren-Regiment   Reitende Artillerie
(1815 Kgl. Preuss. 8. Ulanen-Regiment)   (1815 Kgl. Preuss. 18. und 19. reitende Batterie)

Russisch-Deutsche Legion. II.
1812—1814.

▲ *Russian-German legion in 1812-1814 by Knoitel*

HISTORICAL DESCRIPTION OF THE CLOTHING AND ARMS OF THE RUSSIAN ARMY - A.V. VISKOVATOV
(First English translation by Mark Conrad)

Soldiershop is glad to presents the complete collection of the great job made by A.V. Viskovatov dedicated to the uniforms and weapons belonging to the Russian army during the Napoleonic period, until 1825. The time we considered corresponds to the reigns of two Tzars: Paul I, who reigned since 1769 until his murder on the 23rd of March 1801, and his son Aleksandr Pavlovič Romanov, that with the title of Alexander I, sat on the throne until the 1st December 1825.

Our reprint in based on the original 19th century volumes, to be precise the volumes from 7 to 9 are dedicated to the reign of Paul I; this first part is distributed on 7 volumes, having a numbering from 1 to 7. From number 10 to 18 of the original volumes, the second part is dedicated to the Russian troops under Alexander I. These still being worked on and they will be soon ready, distributed on twenty volumes approximately. Our new edition, the first ever published in English, both on paper and digital format, boasts a large number of color plates, many of them unpublished and coloured by our team of expert artists and scholars of uniformology. Each volume is based on 50/70 plates, always accompanied by the original translated text which describes the uniforms, the organization and the armament of the Russian army of the period.

In this last book of the Napoleonic series we present the Russian temporary forcesof the Napoleonic wars. A unique work in its genre, a must have in any respecting collection!

Aleksandr Vasilevich Viskovatov born 22 April (4 May New Style) 1804, died 27 February (11 March) 1858 in St. Petersburg, Russian military historian. He graduated from the 1st Cadet Corps and served in the artillery, the hydrographic depot of the Naval Ministry, and then in the Department of Military Educational Institutions. He mainly studied historical artifacts and the histories of military units. Viskovatov's greatest work was the Historical Description of the Clothing and Arms of the Russian Army (Vols. 1-30, St. Petersburg, 1841-62; 2nd ed. Vols. 1-34, St. Petersburg - Novosibirsk - Leningrad, 1899-1948). This work is based on a great quantity of archival documents and contains four thousand colored illustrations.

Viskovatov was the author of Chronicles of the Russian Army (Books 1-20, Sr. Petersburg, 1834-42) and Chronicles of the Russian Imperial Army (Parts 1-7, St. Petersburg, 1852). He collected valuable material on the history of the Russian navy which went into A Short Overview of Russian Naval Campaigns and General Voyages to the End of the XVII Century (St. Petersburg, 1864; 2nd edition Moscow, 1946). Together with A.I. Mikhailovskii-Danilevskii he helped prepare and create the Military Gallery in the Winter Palace.

He wrote the historical military inscriptions for the walls of the Hall of St. George in the Great Palace of the Kremlin. (From the article in the Soviet Military Encyclopedia.)

CONTENTS

*

RUSSIAN ARMY- TEMPORARY FORCES
CHANGES IN THE UNIFORMS AND EQUIPMENT OF TEMPORARY FORCES FROM 1801 TO 1825.

A.   Rural Host or Militia, 1806-1807.

B.   Riga Burgher Company, 1806-1807.

C.   Courland Battalion of Volunteer Marksmen, 1807-1809.

D.   Volunteer Regiments, 1806-1808.

E.   Temporary Internal Mass Levy, 1812.

        1) Mass Levy, Region I

        2) Mass Levy, Region II.

        3) Mass Levy, Region III.

F.   Temporary forces formed in 1812, but not part of the Temporary Internal Mass Levy regions.

G.   Flags, Banners, and Regalia of Temporary Forces.

H.   Medals and other distinctions established to reward service, recognize particular military achievements, and commemorate noteworthy military events, during the reign of EMPEROR ALEXANDER I.

Notes

UNIFORMS AND WEAPONS OF TEMPORARY FORCES FORMED IN 1806, 1807, 1812, AND 1813, THEIR FLAGS AND INSIGNIA, AND MEDALS FOR SERVICE, INDIVIDUAL DEEDS, AND CAMPAIGNS, AS ESTABLISHED DURING THE REIGN OF EMPEROR ALEXANDER I.

A) LAND HOST OR MILITIA, 1806 AND 1807.

6 December 1806 – Peasants and other tenant persons designated by a HIGHEST Manifesto of 30 November of this year to be part of a temporary mass levy [*opolchenie*] or Militia [*Militsiya*], also called the *Land Host* [*Zemskoe Voisko*], were ordered to be supplied by their landowners with normal peasant clothing of whatever folk style was used in the region. Neither hair nor beards would be cut [61]. Generals and field and company-grade officers of this militia were prescribed: standard army infantry dress coat of that time, but single breasted, with piping down the front opening, from the opening to the skirts, and on the turnbacks and cuff flaps; dark-green pants, the same color as the coat, with piping down the side seams; white vest and a hat with a green plume. The following distinctions were established:

a) *For commanders-in-chief of regional militias [U glavnokomanduyushchikh oblastnymi militsiyami]* – two gold field-grade officers' epaulettes (Illus. 2512).

b) *For commanders of provincial militias [U komanduyushchikh gubernskimi militsiyami]* – a gold epaulette on the left shoulder and a gold shoulder strap on the right (Illus. 2513).

c) *For commanders of district militias [U komanduyushchikh uezdnymi militsiyami]* – two gold shoulder straps (Illus. 2514).

d) *For chiliarchs [U tysyachnykh nachal'nikov – i.e commanders of 1000]* – a gold epaulette on the left shoulder (Illus. 2515).

e) *For pentakostarchs [U pyatisotennykh nachal'nikov – i.e. commanders of 500]* – a gold shoulder strap on the left shoulder (Illus. 2515).

f) *For hekatonarchs and other junior officers [U sotennykh nachal'nikov (i.e. commanders of 100) i prochikh mladshikh chinovnikov]* – a coat without epaulettes or shoulder straps (Illus. 2516).

Regional, provincial, and district commanders were directed to wear, as they wished, either swords or sabers, but chiliarchs and lesser officers were obligated to have sabers, which throughout the militia had yellow brass hilts and scabbard mountings, or gilt if so desired by the individual. Commanders-in-chief also had the right to wear military uniforms from previous service instead of the militia pattern [62].

In addition to the distinctions set forth above, the following mandatory colors were established for coat collars, cuffs, and piping:

a) *In Region I [Oblast' I-i]* – (St. Petersburg, Novgorod, Tver, Olonets, and Yaroslav provinces) – red (Illus. 2512).

b) *In Region II* – Estonia, Lifland, Courland, and Pskov provinces) – sky blue [*goluboi*] (Illus. 2513).

c) *In Region III* – Vitebsk, Mogilev, Smolensk, and Chernigov provinces) – white (Illus. 2513).

d) *In Region IV* – Moscow, Tula, Kaluga, and Ryazan provinces) – orange (Illus. 2514).

e) *In Region V* – Orel, Kursk, Voronezh, and Kharkov provinces) – pink [*rozovyi*] (Illus. 2514).

f) *In Region IV* – Kiev, Poltava, Kherson, and Yekaterinoslav provinces) – lilac [*lilovyi*] (Illus. 2515).

g) *In Region VII* – Kostroma, Vologda, Nizhnii-Novgorod, and Vyatka provinces) – raspberry [*malinovyi*] (Illus. 2515) [63].

The weapons for lower ranks or *ratniki* ["fighters" – M.C.] were not subject to any kind of rules, but rather they were allowed to be armed according to local resources: their own, old items from arsenals, or old patterns obtaining through voluntary donations. Thus, in neither clothing nor weapons was there uniformity among the *ratniki*. Only the *Imperial Militia Battalion* (included in the the Life-Guards on 22 January 1808) was dressed and armed alike. Its personnel had the following uniforms and weapons:

Private grenadiers – coat [*mundir*] of dark-green cloth, and in the same color: collar, cuffs, cuff flaps, lapels, and skirttail lining and turnbacks; with red cloth piping along the upper edge and sides of the collar, on the cuffs, cuff flaps, and lapels, along the coat's lower edge and on the turnbacks; with red cloth shoulder straps and flat brass buttons. *Pants* – of dark-green cloth, with red cloth piping in the side seams, and sewn-on leather cuffs, each with seven brass buttons. *Shako* – with a small brass single-flame grenade, white cords, red pompon, and a thick black hair plume (Illus. 2517). *Greatcoat* - single-breasted, reaching a little below the knees, of dark-green cloth with a red cloth piping on the upper and side edges of the collar; shoulder straps; brass buttons, nine down the front, two on the shoulder straps, and one in back at the waist (Illus. 2518). When the greatcoat was not being worn, it was rolled and with two leather straps buckled and fastened behind the back, so that it lay on the backpack's upper edge. *Short sword* – somewhat longer than that used in the army, and with a slightly different hilt; blackened scabbard. *Sword knot* – of standard infantry pattern at that time, white, with red slide, acorn, and (above the tassel). *Sword belt* – black, polished, over the shoulder. *Musket* – infantry pattern with a black sling and lock cover. *Bayonet scabbard* in a frog on the sword belt, of black leather with a brass hook and endpiece. *Cartridge pouch* – of the same black leather, without a badge, on a black *crossbelt* worn crosswise with the sword belt. *Backpack* – rectangular, of black leather, worn using two black leather straps over the shoulder and one horizontally across the chest, fitted so that the lower edge almost touched the pouch. *Water flask* – of the same pattern as throughout the infantry; by means of black leather straps it was hung around the collar so that most of it lay against the rolled greatcoat, and a small part of it against the backpack (Illus. 2517). In those cases when a grenadier, in addition to his water flask, also had his mess section's *kettle* [*artel'nyi kotel*] (of red brass, i.e. copper), the latter was fastend by black leather straps on the right side, and the former on the left (Illus. 2518).

Non-commissioned officers in the Grenadier platoon had the same uniforms and arms as private grenadiers and were distinguished by white, black, and orange tassels and bows on their shako cords, woolen pompons with the upper and lower quarters colored black and orange and the side quarters white, and plumes with white tops with an orange stripe. They also carried *canes*, but did not have the galloon on collar and cuffs as was the practice in the permanent forces (Illus. 2519).

Drummers in the Grenadier platoon had, instead of red shoulder straps, dark-green with red piping; red wings on the shoulders; red plume; black hoops and tabs on the drum, and black drumsticks (Illus. 2519).

Privates, non-commissioned and *drummers of the Marksmen Platoon* were distinguished from these same ranks in the Grenadier platoon in not having plumes, and privates and drummers had yellow pompons.

Privates, non-commissioned officers, and drummers of the three Jäger companies had shakos without plumes. Privates had green pompons and were not authorized short swords, instead carrying only bayonet scabbards in the swordbelt frog (Illus. 2520).

Lower ranks of the Artillery half-company in the IMPERIAL Militia Battalion, in addition to the same uniform as lower ranks in the Jäger companies, were all armed with short swords and had red pompons on their shakos. They were given artillery pouches but without a badge and on a black crossbelt, on which were two prickers on small chains, one brass and one iron (Illus. 2521). Many of these men joined from the peasantry, just as in the grenadier and jäger companies, and wore beards from the time the battalion was formed up to February of 1807 when it left Russia to take part in the campaign against the French.

Officers, along with the same colors and cut of uniform as for lower ranks, wore half-sabers [*polusabli*] on a sword belt of black lacquered leather over the right shoulder. Besides the usual officers' distinctions in shako decorations, silver sword knots, and sashes, they wore two gold epaulettes red red cloth backing (Illus. 2522). Before the time the battalion was included in the Guards, officers were not authorized gorgets.

All the uniforms described here were specifically for winter use. For summer, officers as well as lower ranks were to have the linen pants with integral spats used throughout the infantry until 1833 (Illus. 2521).

It is noteworthy that the Imperial Militia Battalion, formed under the direct supervision and control of GRAND DUKE

AND TSESAREVICH CONSTANTINE PAVLOVICH, was in advance of the permanent troops of the Guards, Army, and Garrison in many details of their uniforms and weapons. Thus, while those troops were all wearing short boots, shakos without leather trim or cords, sword belts around the waist, and round backpacks, the Imperial Militia Battalion already had leather pants cuffs, summer pants with integral spats, shakos with leather reinforcement and cords, sword belts over the shoulder, and rectangular backpacks [64].

7 March 1807 – The *Marksmen Battalions [Bataliony Strelkov]* established on this date from *ratniki* of the III, IV, V, and VII Militia regions, were ordered to have the same clothing as the rest of the Militia, but caftan coats (with a standing collar in the region color); pants, and greatcoats of dark or light green peasant cloth, or in case of shortages—dark gray, provided only that battalions have the same color; black cloth neckcloths and black shakos made from first year wool, with a visor of black lacquered leather, black chinstrap, cockade of black ribbon with orange edges fastened behind a brass button by means of black woolen tape, and a worsted pompon and small tassel in the same color as the caftan collar (Illus. 2523). In regard to weapons it was allowed to have old but serviceable muskets from those returned to arsenals by regiments, with black slings. Thus they could be musketeer, jäger, or dragoon muskets, as well as *shtutser* rifles or carbines, provided only that in each battalion they were the same. Short swords and rifle swords [*shtusernye kortiki*] were permitted, and in case of shortages of one or the other—standard musket bayonets. With all these types of firearms leather black front pouches were worn, as used at that time in jäger regiments, on likewise black leather sword belts worn around the waist [65]. Backpacks and water flasks were prescribed to be of jäger patterns, i.e. with black straps, while mess section kettles were like those introduced in the Imperial Militia Battalion. Officers kept the uniforms used throughout the Militia and already described above [66].

14 and 15 March 1807 – With the discharge of two-thirds of the Rural Host and the formation of a *Mobile* or *Serving Militia* from the remaining third, divided into battalions designated by number and province: 1st, 2nd, and 3rd Moscow, 1st and 2nd Kiev, etc.—these battalions kept the same uniforms and weapons as the Militia as a whole, but with greater uniformity [67]. Thus, for example, in the Vladimir Militia all *ratniki* had caftans, *sharovary* pants, and caps of dark-gray cloth. The last item had a black leather visor and a yellow brass cross on the front, under which was the HIGHEST monogram surrounded by a wreath. All *ratniki* had black leather rectangular backpacks with black straps. Pikes [*piki*] were painted black, and their lower end was shaped like a musket butt. At the top was affixed a long and sharp piece of iron, almost an arshin [28 inches] in length and similar to a musket bayonet (Illus. 2524) [68].

The uniforms described here for Marksmen Battalions and Mobile Militia Battalions remained unchanged up to their disbandment on 27 September 1807.

B) RIGA BURGHER COMPANY, 1806-1807.

With the issue of the HIGHEST Manifesto of 30 November 1806 establishing the Militia, the city of Riga, apart from its already long established two mounted Burgher companies (*Bürger-Wache zu Pferde*), formed for internal city guard duties a temporary foot *Burgher company*, also called the *Foot Burgher-Guard (Bürger-Garde zu Fuss)* which was in existence throughout the time of military operations from 1806 to 1807. No special uniforms or weapons were prescribed for it, and its members were only required to be respectably dressed and have sabers at all musters, as well as muskets when on guard duty. Both weapons were issued from the Riga town arsenal. Only the officers had the standard army uniform of that time, and wore epaulettes, gorgets, and shakos—all with the Riga municipal coat-of-arms, along with swords [*shpagi*] on a waist belt trimmed with silver galloon (Illus. 2525) [69]. The Riga coat-of-arms referenced here was as follows: "a stone wall on a sky-blue field, with open gates and a raised iron portcullis; inside the gates is a golden crowned lion's head; on the wall are two towers with gold pennants, in between which are two crossed iron keys, and above them a gold cross and crown; along the sides of the wall can be seen the Russian state coat-of-arms (Illus. 25252a) [70].

C) COURLAND VOLUNTEER MARKSMEN BATTALION, 1807-1809.

At first no particular uniform or arms were prescribed for the *Courland Volunteer Marksmen Battalion [Kurlyandskii batalion Vol'nykh Strelkov]* established on 9 February 1807, and these were obtained as local circumstances allowed, quickly and without uniformity. However, on 20 July 1808, when the battalion was titled the *Courland Jägers*, it was ordered to be uniformed and armed after the example of army jäger regiments, and with such an appearance it continued its existence until 22 October 1809, when it became part of the 1st Finland Regiment [71].

D) VOLUNTEER REGIMENTS, 1806-1808.

From 24 December 1806 to 16 May 1808 the Army of the Dniester included *Volunteer regiments [Volonterskie polki]* of free or unregistered Moldavian and Russian subjects, but these were never completely formed. They numbered three foot and three mounted regiments, and had no prescribed clothing or weapons, but rather wore their own [72].

E) TEMPORARY FORCES FORMED IN 1812 AND INCLUDED IN THE TEMPORARY INTERNAL MASS LEVY REGIONS.

I) MASS LEVY OF REGION I.

a) Moscow Mass Levy.

A *Directive for the formation of Moscow military forces* confirmed by HIGHEST Authority on 15 July 1812 (concerning 3 jäger regiments, 8 cossack foot regiments, and 1 cossack horse regiment) set forth the following in regard to uniforms, weapons, and horse furniture:

Field and company-grade officers have standard army uniforms; those who have the right to wear the uniform in retirement may also wear these. Mounted and foot cossacks and jägers are dressed in gray Russian caftans of peasant cloth. Long *sharavary* pants are made from the same cloth. Russian shirts opening on the side; neckerchief. Cloth forage caps on the head, and Russian boots, good and greased to be proof against moisture, worn over the pants. Caftans must be wide and ample enough for each man to be able to wear a sheepskin coat [*polushubok*] under it. Boots must be roomy enough so that in winter each man can wrap his feet in pieces of cloth [*onuchi*]. Caftans reach to the knees. Anyone who can will have a sash or girdle. The forage cap must be such that in cold weather it can be tied down over the ears and under the beard. Its pattern in each regiment is left to the choice of the commander, but on each of them is to be a cross stamped from brass, beneath which is a monogram of HIS IMPERIAL MAJESTY'S NAME, within an inscription *"Za Veru i Tsarya" ["For Faith and Tsar"]*.

Each man on foot must have a leather or calfskin backpack. Mounted cossacks have, in place of backpacks, valises and sacks for oats. Regimental commanders are to have straps attached to backpacks so they may be worn as in regular forces. In his backpack each man is to have a shirt and two linen underpants [*porty*], so that when not on duty he can walk about without *sharovary* pants; mittens with warm inserts [*varezhki*]; two foot wraps [*portyanki*], and wearing a third; cloth foot wraps [*onuchi*] and spare boots. In addition, there must be enough room left over in the backpack for a three day supply of rusk. Similarly, mounted cossacks are to store items in their valises. Sheepskin coats are to be rolled above the backpack, as greatcoats were previously carried.

Because of the rapid approach of the enemy and the need to take the fastest measures to obtain uniforms and weapons for the mass levy, these orders could not be carried out in their entirety. Therefore, regiments were variously dressed and armed according to local resources. Some of the men [*voiny*] were in gray peasant caftans, others in camelhair *armyak* coats, and still others in sheepskin coats [*tulupy*]. Some had round hats made from first-year wool, others had four-cornered caps, but most wore round gray cloth hats. Most of the jägers had muskets, but many of them, as well as all the foot cossacks, only had pikes. Some were issued infantry short swords while others, probably the majority, had a common everyday ax (Illus. 2526). Horse cossacks were all armed with lances and sabers, and many also had muskets or carbines (Illus. 2527). The clothing of mass levy *voiny* from the *merchant and townspeople class* was all dark green. They had tall round hats trimmed with black fleece. (Illus. 2528). *Officers* with these forces, in order to achieve a certain uniformity of appearance with the men, wore dark-green uniform frock coats [*syurtuki*] with a likewise dark-green collar, and the same hats as the *voiny* (Illus. 2528) [73].

Graf Saltykov's Hussars and Graf Dmitriev-Mamonov's Cossacks were regiments raised on the initiative of those individuals to reinforce the Moscow forces, and had the clothing and weapons appropriate to those types of cavalry:

Graf Saltykov's Regiment – shakos with yellow cords and pompon and brass fittings; black pelisses, dolmans, and sabertaches, with yellow braid and lace and brass buttons; raspberry collars and cuffs on the dolmans, raspberry *chakchiry* pants with yellow trim and tracery; yellow girdles with likewise yellow tassels and black slides; black saddlecloths with a raspberry toothed edge and yellow cord and monograms (Illus. 2529). Officers were distinguished by gold braid, galloon, buttons, and other metal appointments, with silver shako cords and girdles of mixed with black and orange silk (Illus. 2529).

Graf Dmitriev-Mamonov's Regiment – all uniform clothing was dark green with turquoise distinctions and gold appointments; the fur on lower ranks' hats was black sheepskin, but on officers'—bearskin (Illus. 2530).

Shakos in Graf Saltykov's Regiment and the headdresses in Graf Dmitriev-Mamonov's had the same crosses and monograms as related above for the Moscow mass levy's jäger and cossack regiments [74].

b) TVER Mass Levy.

In regard to clothing and weapons for the Tver Mass levy (5 foot cossack regiments and 1 horse) the same directive was followed as for Moscow, but for the same reasons its initial objectives could not be fully met. The Tver Mass levy was distinguished from Moscow's only in replacing tall caps and hats with military-style forage caps with a visor and, as in Moscow, cross and monogram made from sheet brass (Illus. 2531) [75].

c) YAROSLAV Mass Levy.

This *opolchenie* (4 foot cossack regiments and 1 horse), like that of Tver, was guided in matters of dress and arms by the directive for the Moscow military forces, but as to whether it complied in all details or with certain deviations—no information has been preserved [76].

d) VLADIMIR Mass Levy.

Private cossacks of the Vladimir Mass levy (6 foot cossack regiments) had dark-gray cloth caftans tied with girdles of the same material; dark-gray cloth netherwear [*nizhnee plat'e*]; dark-gray cloth hats 5 vershoks [8-3/4 inches] tall, with the same decoration and the mass-levies above; dark-gray cloth backpacks with likewise gray cloth straps instead of leather; pikes, for the most part from the Vladimir Militia of 1807, i.e. with a musket-like butt at one end and a long iron point at the other (Illus. 2532). *Uryadniki (non-commissioned officers)* were distinguished by silver lace sewn onto the caftan collar as well as by being armed with sabers in addition to a pike. *Field* and *company-grade officers* at first wore the uniforms of those regiments and corps in which they previousl served, but because of the great diversity in appearance that ensued, they later all received a common uniform of cossack-like style, of very dark-blue cloth with gold epaulettes, red piping along the edge of the right side of the front, as well as along the upper and side edges of the collar, which was further trimmed along all four sides with flat black silk cord, like the embroidery on hussar collars. Pants, also dark green, had red cloth trim (*lampasy* stripes) and piping; Very dark-blue forage caps, of standard officers' pattern, with red piping and the same cross and monogram as in the mass-levies above. With this uniform, officers had sabers in scabbards with iron mountings (brass only in the 3rd Regiment), with a brass or gilded hilt, on a sword belt trimmed with gold galloon. They had cavalry officers' sword knots and silver officers' sashes (Illus. 2532) [77].

e) RYAZAN Mass levy.

The *foot opolchenie* of Ryazan Province (2 jäger regiments and 4 foot cossack regiments) was like that of Vladimir in regard to colors and patterns, and the regiments were distinguished among themselves by the colors of the collar, hat band, and *sharavary* pants stripes and piping: 1st Foot Cossack Regiment—raspberry, 3rd—sky blue (Illus. 2533). The colors for the other foot regiments are unknown. The edges of the collar, cuffs, and caftan skirts were trimmed with cloth piping of the same color, i.e. dark gray, and along with this the caftan coat was tied at the waist with a black leather belt. Like the jägers, the foot cossacks were armed only with pikes, and the former received muskets only in 1813 when they were already outside Russia. The *Horse Cossack Regiment* had jackets instead of caftan coats, with red collars. The band on the forage cap was also red, as well as the stripes and piping on the *sharavary* pants. This regiment wore caps without visors, and was armed only with lances and sabers (Illus. 2533). There was the same variety in horse furniture as in other provinces' mass levies. The Ryazan mass levy's infantry had backpacks of leather, calfskin, or—in case neither of these were available—linen canvas, while cavalry had gray cloth valises. In regard to uniforms and weapons for officers the only information that has been preserved is that they carried sabers on a black leather sword belt, with a silver sword knot. In June and July of 1813, when the Ryazan mass levy was outside Russia, near Dresden, it received new uniforms similar to those for Army regiments, but no details are known [78].

f) TULA Mass levy.

Of all the temporary forces formed in 1812, the Tula *opolchenie* (1 jäger regiment, 4 foot cossack regiments, 2 horse cossack regiments, and 2 half-companies of horse artillery) had the most information preserved. Uniforms for *jägers* of this mass levy were similar to that described above for Ryazan province, but with collar, cuffs, and pants trim all of black cloth, without piping. They had green wool girdles. Forage caps were gray with a black band and a black lacquered visor, and on the front were a cross and the HIGHEST monogram. The first rank of the regiment had muskets with black slings, black leather pouches on black crossbelts, and bayonet scabbards on a black leather sword belt (Illus. 2534). In addition to a musket, many men also had a saber, others broad swords, and still others short swords. Some had plain axes. Some of the jägers were issued cartridge pouches on black belts, and the rest put their cartridges in pockets cut in the backpack. For all personnel the backpacks themselves were of gray cloth with black straps crossing over the chest. *Officers'* uniforms were of the same style as for lower ranks, but the caftan coats were very dark gray, almost black, with gold epaulettes and a green silk girdle. Light-gray *sharavary* pants with wide black stripes and piping; dark-gray forage caps with a black visor, on which was embroidered in gold the words "*Za veru i Tsarya*" ["*For the faith and the Tsar*]. Sabers were on black leather sword belts trimmed with gold galloon; silver infantry sword knots and silver sashes (Illus. 2534). *Generals'* uniforms were distinguished by having standard gold general officers' embroidery on the coat's collar and cuffs. *Foot cossack regiments* were distinguished from jägers by their headdress, which for them was of standard cossack style but without a bag, of the same cloth as the caftan coat, and with a black chinstrap. These cossacks had the same accouterments as jägers and were armed with muskets in the first rank and with pikes in the others (Illus. 2535). The regiments were distinguished by their shoulder straps: red in the 1st Regiment, white in the 2nd, sky blue in the 3rd, and dark blue in the 4th. *Non-commissioned officers [uryadniki]* were distinguished by gold galloon on the collar and brass chinscales on the headdress, and had sabers (Illus. 2535).

Officers were distinguished from their counterparts in the Jäger regiment by their headdress, which for them was of the pattern prescribed for private cossacks but with a black cloth bag. It had a gilded cross and monogram, likewise gilded chinscales, and silver cords (Illus. 2535). They also wore forage caps as in the Jäger regiment. Cords (whitened) were also prescribed for lower ranks but because of the circumstance of that time were not able to be made before the regiments marched off. *Horse cossacks* were clothed in the same style as those on foot (with red shoulder straps in the 1st Regiment and white in the 2nd). They had pouches of black leather with an iron ramrod attached to the cover. The pouch crossbelt was of the same leather. They were armed with sabers with a leather sword knot; pistols at the waist, and lances. For the most part horse furniture was non-uniform, but many had cossack saddles with deep pillows and, over them, black leather , with cruppers and chestbands [*pakhvyami i popers'yami*]; reins had a lead [*chumbur*]; round leather valises fastened behind the saddle (Illus. 2536). *Officers* had caftan coats with white lining, boots with spurs, sabers with a cavalry officer's sword knot, silver sashes, and black lacquered pouches on a similar crossbelt that had gilt badges on the front with similarly gilt chains: two for prickers and one for a ramrod (Illus. 2537). The pouch lid had a gilt representation of the HIGHEST monogram. The uniform for *Generals* was distinguished by epaulettes and the gold embroidery prescribed for general officer rank. All officers had black cossack saddlecloths with trim either of gold galloon or yellow woolen tape (Illus. 2537). The uniforms, accouterments, weapons, and horse furniture for *Horse-Artillery* half-companies was almost the same as for horse cossacks, but without lances and with the addition of two crossed cannons and a single-flame grenade on the headdress below the monogram, and with red piping on the collar, cuffs, and between the pants stripes. *Combatant lower ranks* had two prickers with chains on the pouch crossbelt, following the example throughout the artillery. One pricker was brass, the other iron. The men riding with the guns and caissons had short swords of the pattern for pioneers at that time, while the rest had sabers with leather sword knots like those in the horse cossack regiments. *Uryadniki* did not have prickers on their pouch belts (Illus. 2538), while *officers* and *supernumery officers [za-uryad-ofitsery]* (from students from the Tula Alexander Nobles School) [*Tul'skoe Aleksandrovskoe Dvoryanskoe uchilishche*] had the same distinctions from lower ranks as were in the horse cossack regiments (Illus. 2539). When not in formation they wore the same forage caps as jäger officers in the Tula Mass Levy, but with the addition of a red edge to the top of the cap band (Illus. 2539) [79].

In 1813, when passing through Kovno, the second and third ranks in all the Tula Mass Levy's foot regiments, both jägers and cossacks, had their pikes replaced by muskets. In the same year, in the months of June and July, the 1st Horse Cossack Regiment had black uniform clothing made up in place of the gray, and in regard to this it received jackets instead of caftans (Illus. 2540). Officers also wore jackets during parades and reviews, and at other times were in caftan coats [80].

g) KALUGA MASS LEVY.

Uniforms and weapons for this *opolchenie* (1 jäger battalion, 5 foot cossack regiments, and 1 horse cossack regiment) were based on the instructions for Moscow military forces, but details are not known [81].

h) SMOLENSK MASS LEVY.

Ratniki of this *opolchenie* did not form individual regiments, and while most were on foot, some were mounted. They were clothed and armed exactly following the example of the Moscow mass levy's foot and horse cossacks. As for officers, some wore standard army coats while others kept the uniforms they had when they retired from service [82].

II) MASS LEVY OF REGION II.

a) ST.-PETERSBURG MASS LEVY.

This *opolchenie* consisted of 15 foot *druzhinas* and 2 horse cossack regiments. In regard to uniforms and weapons of the *druzhinas* the HIGHEST confirmed *Regulation on the composition of St.-Petersburg military forces*, 27 August 1812, set fort the following directives.

In the infantry all field and company-grade officers serving in the mass levy are to have standard army uniforms. Those

▲ *Russian Generals 1812-14*

who have uniforms from the time they entered retirement may also wear those. Foot soldiers keep their peasant dress, but caftans may not be longer than one vershok [1-3/4 inches] below the knees. Other parts of their dress are according to their means. Cloth forage cap as headgear. Black boots with similar shanks that in fall and during cold weather may be worn over the *sharavary* pants. The boots must be made so that in winter the man can wrap his feet in cloth wrappings. Caftans must be of a width so that a man may wear a sheepskin coat under it. Anyone who is able may wear a cloth belt, or girdle. The forage cap must be such that during cold weather a man can tie it down over his ears and under the chin. The pattern for the cap is laid down to be the same for everyone, and each one is to have a cross pressed out of brass [*mednaya latun'*]. On the cross is the monogram name of HIS IMPERIAL MAJESTY and the inscription "*Za veru i Tsarya*" ("For Faith and Tsar" – this inscription was placed in the following manner: on the right arm of the cross were the word "*Za Veru*" pressed in relief, and on the left--"*i Tsarya*"). Each foot soldier is to have a backpack containing one shirt, linen long johns, mittens with warm inserts, two socks, cloth foot wraps, and spare boots. In addition, there must be enough space left in the backpack for three-day supply of rusk. Men in the *druzhinas* are to make carrying straps for the backpacks following the example of regular troops. For arms they are prescribed muskets. A leather pouch for cartridges is to be worn over the shoulder, of whatever pattern that can be obtained. For each man cartridges with bullets: 40 in the pouch and 35 in a box. Foot soldiers do not have sabers or short swords. It is not permitted to add special collars or alter the pattern or style of peasants' and townspeople's caftans. *Druzhina* commanders are allowed to have the *druzhina* number on their personnel, sewn in cloth or made from tape, on the right breast of the caftan.

In actuality, all foot *druzhinas* of the St.-Petersburg mass levy had clothing and forage caps made of gray cloth (Illus. 2541) without any numbers sewn onto the coats, except for the 1st Druzhina which was made up of merchants and townsmen and had green uniforms (Illus. 2541). All fifteen *druzhinas* were armed with muskets (imported from England) and common everyday axes, which in the 1st Druzhina were carried in a frog on a black leather belt worn crosswise over a similar pouch belt, but in other *druzhinas* were simply thrust into the girdle. Soon after the capture of Polotsk in October of 1812, all members of the mass levy gave up their axes and were left only with muskets. *Non-commissioned officers [uryadniki]* were distinguished from plain or private soldiers by a red band and the same colored piping on the forage cap; a black leather belt fastened in front with a buckle, and a saber or short sword on a black leather belt over the right shoulder. Over the left shoulder they had a leather pouch on the same kind of belt, and were armed partly with muskets and partly with carbines (Illus. 2542). In parade dress *officers* wore the standard army tailcoat, as prescribed, but almost always they were seen in an army infantry frock coat, gray riding trousers with red piping on the outer seams and black leather reinforcement on the inner seams, and a dark-green forage cap with a red band, red piping, and black leather visor. When on campaign they had sashes and black leather backpacks with similar straps (Illus. 2543). In the summer of 1813, when at Danzig, all *druzhinas* received clothing made from dark-green Prussian cloth and matching forage caps with red bands (Illus. 2544). Even earlier, in spring of that same year at the start of the blockade of Danzig, when its own mass levy was being formed in Prussia and whose officers had gray cossack-style coats [*kazakiny*] and forage caps with gold crosses and the inscription "Mit Gott für König," many officers of the St.-Petersburg *druzhinas* adopted the same frock coats and sewed to their caps crosses with the Cyrillic inscription "*Za Veru i Tsarya*" (Illus. 2545). This was by their own choice, even if the authorities decided to allow it, and although there was no established pattern, these continued to be worn right up to the return of the mass levy to St. Petersburg in 1814 [83].

The St.-Petersburg mass levy's mounted regiments, titled the *1st and 2nd Cossack Regiments*, and also called the *1st and 2nd Volunteer Regiments*, had caftan coats in cossack style and *sharavary* pants, and black fur headdresses. These had white cords for lower ranks, with a white hair plume, black chinstrap without scales, and a black leather visor without edging, while for officers these had silver cords, a white hair plume, chinscales the same color as the buttons, and a metallic edge to the visor, again the same color as the buttons. All ranks wore boots with spurs. *In the 1st Regiment* the uniform was black with light-blue [*svetlosinii*] or sky-blue [*goluboi*] collar, pointed cuffs, and pants trim. Braid was made from white thread (silver for officers), and consisted of cords on the chest. White buttons (Illus. 2546 and 2546a). *In the 2nd Regiment* the uniform was very dark blue [*temnosinii*] with raspberry collar, cuffs, and trim. For officers the sewn-on braid was black cord with likewise black buttons, while lower ranks had no braid (Illus. 2546 and 2546a). All officers had epaulettes, and lower ranks—worsted cords, white in the 1st Regiment and black in the 2nd. In the 1st Regiment the shako for all ranks was of bearskin with a white (same as the buttons) human skull over two crossed bones. In the 2nd shakos were of bearskin for officers but sheepskin for lower ranks, both with a HIGHEST monogram beneath a crown.

(*Note*: Due to these shako badges, both regiments were popularly known by nicknames: the 1st (originally formed by Graf Doleiver, succeeded by Colonel Yakhontov) was the *Deathdealers [Smertonosnyi]* or *Immortals [Bezsmertnyi]*, while the 2nd (formed by Staff-Captain Baron Bode) was *Alexander's [Aleksandriiskii]*. Although both regiments were actually cossack, the simularity of parts of their uniforms to those of hussars, specifically the cords on the chest, lead to them often being called hussar regiments.)

Horse furniture was lancer pattern, and the regiments differed in the color of the saddlecloth: black with sky blue or light blue in the 1st, and dark blue with raspberry trim, piping, monograms, and crowns in the 2nd [84].

b) NOVGOROD MASS LEVY.

This *opolchenie*, consisting of 12 foot *druzhinas* and active throughout the war of 1812, '13, and '14 along with the St.-Petersburg mass levy, was identical to it in regard to uniforms and weapons [85].

III) MASS LEVY OF REGION III.

The commander of this *opolchenie*, Lieutenant General Graf Tolstoi, established a single common uniform and the same weapons and horse furniture for all its members:

For foot soldiers:

...gray camelhair *armyak* coat, also called a *chepan*, trousers or *sharavary* pants of gray cloth, with a belt [*oshkurka*], and able to be worn tucked into the boots during inclement weather; neck cloth, leather belt with buckle in place of a girdle; leather cartridge box for 20 rounds, worn on a leather girdle; boots with blunt toes, wide and reaching to the knee so that in bad weather the pants may be tucked into them; leather backpack with two straps; cloth cap on which is a cross pressed out of brass, with the SOVEREIGN EMPOROR'S monogram below; sheepskin half-coats able to cover the lower stomach.

For horse soldiers:

...gray camelhair *armyak* coat, or *chepan*; pants as for the infantry; neck cloth, cap as for the infantry; belt with buckle instead of girdle; leather pouch for 10 cartridges, worn on a waistbelt; boots able to have the pants tucked into them in bad weather; sheepskin half-coat as for the infantry; valise; saddle with stirrup straps [*putlishcha*], crupper [*popers'e*], lining [*podlogon'e*], valise straps on the rear arch and two on the front arch for the half-coat, and iron stirrups; bridle with forehead strap [*nalobnik*], chinstrap [*podborodnik*], and lead [*chumbur*]; linen sacks and bags tied to the rear arch, and two pairs of horseshoes.

Additionally, both foot and mounted personnel are to have water flasks with straps. For foot and horse personnel it is not prohibited to have cloth cossack jackets with sleeves, covering the soldier's chest. [86].

This regulation was not strictly carried out, and the mass levy of Region III had clothing, arms, and horse furniture as follows:

a) NIZHNII-NOVGOROD MASS LEVY.

This *opolchenie* (5 foot regiments and 1 horse) was clothed at its formation according to Graf Tolstoi's regulation, with four-cornered caps of lancer pattern, with a band of black sheep's fleece. *Foot soldiers* were armed with pikes with a wide flat point (Illus. 2547), while *horse soldiers* had normal lances sabers and cossack shabracks of gray cloth with red trim and monograms. They were further distinguished from foot troops by having a gray cloth band on the cap instead of fleece, with two rows of red cloth piping. The same piping was along the top and bottom edges of the collar, on the cuffs, and along the front opening; gray cloth girdles with red cloth piping along the edges, with similar trim on the *sharavary* pants, in one row (Illus. 2547). In 1813, when the Nizhnii-Novgorod mass levy as over the border, *soldiers in foot regiments* received caftan coats and trousers of the previous pattern but in green, and similar cloth girdles, all with piping or trim of red cloth as for mounted soldiers in 1812. Along with this new uniform they were given infantry shakos of the current pattern, with cords and pompons, muskets, short swords, pouches, and accouterments (Illus. 2548). *Horse soldiers* received gray jackets with a red collar, lapels, and piping on the cuffs; yellow buttons; red girdles and a red band on the cap, to which was added a gray pompon. Horse soldiers kept all their previous weapons with a small red and white pennant added to the lance (Illus. 2548) [87]. No information has been preserved regarding officers' uniforms in the Nizhnii-Novgorod mass levy.

b) KOSTROMA MASS LEVY.

This *opolchenie* (4 regiments and 1 battalion on foot, and 1 horse regiment) was uniformed and armed after the manner of the Nizhnii-Novgorod mass levy with the sole difference that in 1813, when over the border, *horse* soldiers received dark-green jackets of lancer pattern but without tails, with orange collar, lapels, and cuffs, with yellow buttons and white epaulettes; orange girldes with yellow trim; gray riding trousers with orange stripes and piping; gray caps of lancer pattern, with black leather above and an orange band, on which in front over the visor was a triangular badge of yellow brass with the HIGHEST monogram pressed in relief, and a brass cross above the band, with white cords and pompon; black lancer saddlecloths trimmed with two rows of orange cloth. On the fronts of these saddlecloths were sewn HIGHEST monograms of yellow cord, and in the back a coat of arms in the form of a shield divided into quarters: left top—light blue or sky blue, with a yellow half moon turned downward; right top—yellow; left bottom—orange, both without figures; right botton—white with a yellow crown. (*Note:* This is what is depicted on preserved drawings. The significance of this coat of arms is unknown.) (Illus. 2549). Along with this same uniform and horse furniture, and in addition to their usual distinctions, *officers* differed from lower ranks in having dark-green *chakchiry* trousers instead of gray (Illus. 2549) [88].

c) SIMBIRSK MASS LEVY.

This *opolchenie* (4 foot and 1 horse regiment) was like the Nizhnii-Novgorod in regard to the uniforms for *foot* and *horse* soldiers except that instead of four-cornered caps with fleece bands, it had regular round forage caps of gray cloth, with a black leather visor, and turquoise piping on the collar, cuffs, and around the entire caftan coat, as well as on the side seams of the *sharavary* pants (Illus. 2550). *Officers* wore all the same uniform as prescribed for lower ranks, but with the collar, cuffs, epaulette field, and forage-cap band made from turquoise cloth. All of them had sabers on a black sword belt (Illus. 2551). In 1813 *foot regiments* received muskets in place of pikes, while the *horse regiment* was given completey new cossack style uniforms. These were very dark blue with turquoise collar, cuffs, piping down the front and around the edges of the shoulder straps, trim on the girdle, *sharavary* pants stripes and piping, and bag on the headdress. Around the entire collar and along the edges of the cuffs and front opening were sewn two rows of thin flat yellow cord. All horse soldiers had on their headdress a white hair plume and likewise white cords, as well as boots with spurs, asaber on a black belt, a pouch on the right side and a pistol on the left—both on black crossbelts, and a lance with a black shaft and a pennant with a turquoise upper half and white below (Illus. 2552). Horse furniture was as standard for cossacks but with hussar saddlecloths of dark-green cloth, with turquoise trim and yellow monograms. *Officers of the horse regiment* received uniforms of the same pattern as for soldiers but all trim was of thin gold cord, and headdresses had a plume of cock feathers, chinscales, and a visor, the last having a gilt edging on its outside. They were prescribed army hussar officer pattern sabers, sword knots, sword belts (black with gold galloon), pouches, pouch belts (black with gold galloon and silver mountings), sashes, and—for parades—waist-length jackets that were otherwise similar to the caftan coat (Illus. 2552) [89].

d) PENZA MASS LEVY.

The foot soldiers of this *opolchenie*, part of District III and consisting of 4 foot and 1 horse regiment, were dressed in peasant *chepan* or *kaftan* coats of gray cloth, and likewise gray *sharavary* pants worn over the boots. Each man was to have a neckcloth of any personally chosen color. The coat was girded with a gray cloth sash over which was a black leather strap with buckle. Soldiers in the foot regiments wore gray cloth headdresses shaped like a shako, with a black leather visor. On these was pressed brass cross, the monogram of EMPEROR ALEXANDER I, and an elongated badge in the shape of a ribbon with the Cyrillic inscription *"Za Veru i Tsarya."* Part of these men were armed with muskets and the other with pikes. Those with muskets wore a black leather cartridge pouch in front, for 20 rounds, affixed to the waistbelt (Illus. 2553). Some had sabers, others short swords, and all were provided with rectangular backpacks of black leather, worn on two black straps crossing over the chest, as well as water flasks of white tin, worn on a black leather strap over the left shoulder. Soldiers in the horse regiment were dressed just as those on foot except for the addition to the caftan coat of a small white cloth collar and similar cuffs. They all had sabers and the same kind of cartridge pouch and water flask as the foot soldiers. The flask was attached to a black strap worn over the left shoulder.

Most of the men were armed with a lance and a pistol stored in a black leather holster attached to the waistbelt at the left side (Illus. 2554). Some, but not many, had a carbine instead of the pistol.

Every man had a valise of gray cloth attched to the read saddle arch, and all horse furniture was like that of cossacks.

Apart from the clothing described here, neither foot nor mounted soldiers were prohibited from having cloth cossack jackets obtained on their own. Officers who had been retired without the right to wear a uniform, as well as officers who previously had been justs civil officials, had the standard army dress coat, while officers who had left the service with the right to wear the uniform wore those.

In the summer of 1813, when the Penza mass levy was outside Russia, it received uniforms of a new pattern, but no information has been preserved as to what it was exactly [90].

e) KAZAN MASS LEVY, JOINED WITH THE VYATKA MASS LEVY.

The uniform of this *opolchenie* (1 regiment and 1 battalion of foot and 3 horse sotnias) was in complete conformance with that established by Lieutenant General Graf Tolstoi for the District III mass levy, described above. With it, all soldiers wore the same caps as the foot component of the Simbirsk mass levy, and had: *foot*—muskets and cartridge pouches on a waistbelt, and *horse*—lances (Illus. 2555) [91].

F) TEMPORARY FORCES FORMED IN 1812 BUT NOT PART OF THE DISTRICTS OF THE TEMPORARY INTERNAL MASS LEVY.

a) HER IMPERIAL HIGHNESS GRAND DUCHESS CATHERINE PAVLOVNA'S BATTALION.

This battalion, armed as the army jäger regiments of that time, also had similar uniforms, but all dark green without piping. Long breeches [*bryuki*] or pants [*sharavary*] were worn over boots; shakos were trimmed with fur—dog for lower ranks and bearskin for officers—with the monogram of EMPEROR ALEXANDER I in front. With this officers wore gold guards epaulettes and sabers in scabbards with gilt mountings, hung over the shoulder on top of the coat on a sword belt of black lacquered leather (Illus. 2556) [92].

b) SQUADRON OF KHERSON PROVINCIAL LANDOWNER SKARZHINSKII.

Privates, or *cossacks*, of this squadron had white cloth jackets without tails, with a sky-blue collar, lapels, and cuffs; white piping on the collar and along all seams; sky-blue piping on the shoulder straps; white buttons; very dark blue *sharovary* pants with one sky-blue stripe outlined with a white edges; white girdles with sky-blue stripes; cossack headdresses with a sky-blue top and white cords; boots with spurs; sabers with iron hilts, in black scabbards with some iron mountings in places; pistols thrust in the girdle; pouches and pouch belts of black leather; lances with a black shaft; cossack horse furniture, with a sky-blue shabrack trimmed with white tape or white cloth (Illus. 2557). Cossacks in the rear rank, in addition to the above weapons, also had carbines held by a black elkskin strap worn over the right shoulder. *Officers'* uniforms had the same colors and pattern as the lower ranks, with silver epaulettes, headdress cords, sashes, and sword knots, and headdresses with bearskin (Illus. 2557) [93].

c) CHERNIGOV MASS LEVY.

Cossacks in this *opolchenie* (8 three-battalion horse regiments and 1 composite battalion) had dark-green jackets with red piping and yellow regimental numbers on the shoulder straps; dark-green *sharavary* pants, with a single red stripe; black sheepskin headdresses with a red bag, white cords, and a black woolen plume; deerskin gloves with small guantlet cuffs; sabers with iron hilts, likewise iron open frame on the scabbards; black sword belts; black leather waistbelt 4 vershoks [7 inches] wide, with a cartridge box and two pistol holsters; two pistols each, on black cords; cartridge pouches of white tin with a brass two-headed eagle on the lid; black cartridge-pouch crossbelts (over the left shoulder), with white metal fittings; normal cossack *nagaika* whips thrust in the waistbelt on the left side; lance on black shafts 4 arshins [9 feet 4 inches] long, with a tricolor pennant: blue [*svetlosinii*] above, red middle, and white below. Horse furniture was as standard for cossacks, with a dark-gray cloth shabrack without any trim or decoration, and with a dark-blue cloth and fleece coat on the front saddle arch (when not being worn by the cossack) (Illus. 2558) [94].

d) POLTAVA MASS LEVY.

This *opolchenie*, which consisted of horse and foot cossacks, had two types of uniforms and weapons: horse and foot. *Horse cossacks* were dressed in dark-blue cossack jackets with red collars and cuffs, and in dark-blue *sharavary* pants with red stripes and piping; they wore black woolen girdles and had cossack headdresses of black astrakhan with a red cloth bag, white cords, white pompons, black hair plumes, brass chinscales, and a brass monogram of EMPEROR ALEXANDER I within laurels and under a crown. Arms and accouterments were the same as for the Chernigov mass levy, but sword belts were of red Russia leather and the flank cossacks in each platoon additionally had carbines carried on black leather bandoleers. Along with the same horse furniture as in the Cherginov mass levy, Poltava horse cossacks had dark-blue saddlecloths with red cloth trim and HIGHEST monograms (Illus. 2559). *Non-commissisoned officers* had plumes with white tops (Illus. 2559). *Officers* had jackets for parades and caftan coats for normal wear. They were distinguished by flat silver cord sewn on the collar, cuffs, and along the front opening, in the same style as the Simbirsk mass levy. They wore silver epaulettes, headdresses with silver cords, pompon, edging on the visor, and white plume; hussar officers' sabers, sword belts, cartridge pouches with silver fittings, silver sword knots, and silver sashes. Their saddlecloths were trimmed with red cloth as well as silver galloon, and had likewise silver monograms and crowns (Illus. 2560). *Lower ranks* of the Poltava mass levy's foot component had, instead of jackets, short gray caftan coats reaching to above the knee; gray *sharavary* pants, and headdresses of the Don cossack pattern, with a gray bag (Illus. 2561). At first their weaponry consisted solely of pikes, but later also muskets, along with which they received cartridge pouches on a black belt. With both the pike and the musket they had infantry short sword on a black belt worn around the waist. *Officers* wore silver epaulettes and headdresses of black fleece, with a red top (Illus. 2561) [95].

e) VOLOGDA AND OLONETS MASS LEVY.

This *opolchenie*, which consisted of marksmen [*strelki*], was primarily drawn from indigineous Zyryan bird and animal hunters in Yarensk, and Ust-Sysolsk districts. They were prescribed to "have normal peasant clothing such as: cloth Russian caftan [*kaftan*], European coat [*kamzol*], or warm coat [*fufaika*], trousers [*shtany*], thick boots with foot wrappings, three shirts with pants [*porty*], hat or cap, neckerchief, and short fur coat for autumn. It is only required that all be of stout construction and not old or worn out. Each man is to have a musket of the kind using in the territory for hunting animals." [96]

Later, when joined with the St.-Petersburg mass levy, the *opolchenie* of Vologda and Olonets was uniformed in the same way: gray cloth coats of cossack style, similar pants, and gray forage caps with a black visor and brass cross. Along with this, instead of a girdle, they belted their waists with a black leather strap with a brass buckle in front. They had gray cloth greatcoats and black accouterments of jäger pattern (Illus. 2562) [97]. In 1813 this mass levy was uniformed exactly like that of St. Petersburg and Novgorod, i.e. in greenish-blue caftan coats, *sharavary* pants, and forage caps [98].

f) LIEUTENANT NIROT'S VOLONTEER MARKSMEN CORPS.

No information has been preserved regarding the uniforms and weapons of the *Volunteer Corps of Mounted Marksmen [Volonterskii Korpus konnykh strelkov]* which was in existence from 16 April 1812 throughout the duration of the Patriotic War. It was formed from the nobility of the Baltic provinces on the initiative of retired Lieutenant Nirot. It is known only that this corps was ordered to follow "the example of light irregular cossack troops." [99]

g) COURLAND CORPS OF MARKSMEN.

Neither is any information recorded regarding the uniforms and weapons of the *Courland Corps of Marksmen [Korpus Kurlayndskikh strelkov]*, established 12 June 1812 and recruited from Courland forest warden settlements [*Bushvekhterskiya seleniya*, c.f. German *Buschwächter*]. It is known only that privates, called Forest Jägers [*Forsht-yegeri*], were all mounted, and officers and non-commissioned officers were officials assigned from the Forestry administration [*Lesnoe vedomstvo*] [100].

h) CORPS OF LIVONIAN VOLUNTEER HORSE AND FOOT JÄGERS.

In regard to this corps [*Korpus vol'nykh konnykh i peshikh Liflyandskikh yegerei*], a relevant regulation of 2 August 1812 shows only that the one horse and two foot companies that comprised it were armed with: the first—broad swords, muskets with bayonets, and pistols, and the latter—daggers and muskets with bayonets. Also, that all the companies had cartridge pouches. What their uniform was remains unknown [101].

i) LIVONIA COSSACK REGIMENT.

On 23 October 1812 this regiment, consisting of two foot battalions, was prescribed: dark-blue cloth caftan coat with red lining; dark-blue *sharavary* pants with leather reinforcement, and leather cartridge pouches. There is no information on other parts of the uniform or weapons [102].

In regard to clothing and arms for other Temporary forces formed in 1812 and 1813, such as *Lieutenant Colonel Diebitsch's force [otryad Podpolkovnika Dibicha]* (formed from prisoners), the *Riga Burgher Companies [Rizhskiya Birgerskiya roty]*, and the *Russo-German Legion [Rossiisko-Germanskii Legion]*, no information of any kind has been preserved except that uniforms for lower ranks of the Legion were ordered to be made from recruit cloth, with yellow, sky-blue, or red collars [103].

G) FLAGS, BANNERS, AND REGALIA OF THE 1807 RURAL HOST OR MILITIA, AND THE 1812 INTERNAL MASS LEVY.

I) *Flags of the 1807 Rural Host.*

In 1807 *flags* were prepared for battalions of the Mobile or Serving militia, but due to the quickly concluded peace treaty with France, they were not issued to the battalions. They had a cross in the center and the inscription *"For Faith and Fatherland" ["Za Veru i Otechestvo"]*. Some of these flags were white with raspberry cross and inscription, others were raspberry of a more or less dark shade, with white, yellow, orange, sky-blue, and green crosses, and white letters. On the field of the flag, at three edges, was sewn silver or white fringe, and to the top of the pole (of no specified color) was affixed a brass outline of spearhead with a cross in the center (Illus. 2563) [104]. It is not known for which militia battalions these flags were intended, nor in what numbers for each.

II) *Flags, banners, and regalia of the 1812 Internal Mass Levy.*

Of the number of mass levies called out in 1812, some were provided with new, specifically made *flags [znamena]*. Others, instead of flags, received *banners [khorugvi]* from local churches, and still others had only other *regalia [znachki]*. All of these, insofar as is known from surviving information, were as follows:

a) MOSCOW MASS LEVY.

Two banners, raspberry in color, with gold crosses, sun rays, stars, and other figures, and with gold edges. On one of the banners are depicted the Ascension of Our Lord and the Assumption of the Mother of God (Illus. 2564), and on the other—the Transfiguration of Our Lord and Saint Nicholas (Illus. 2565). The second of these banners has a silver fringe around it [105].

b) THIRD FOOT COSSACK REGIMENT, RYAZAN MASS LEVY.

A light-green flag with green fringes, having on each side in the center a rectangle surrounded by a light sky-blue [*svetlogoluboi*] border, with gold stripes or edging. On one of these rectangles is a painted image of the Saving of the Image Not Created by Human Hands, with the gold Cyrillic words on the edge, *"The Lord provides and we do not want" ["Gospod' nas paset nichtozhe lishit"]*; on the other, dark sky-blue [*temnogoloboi*] rectangle is painted in gold the monogram name of EMPEROR ALEXANDER I, without a crown, and with the gold inscription on the edge *"III regiment of the Ryazan mass levy in the year 1812" ["III polka Ryazanskago opolcheniya 1812 goda"]*. The pole, the same color as the flag, has a hollow gilt spearhead with EMPEROR ALEXANDER I's monogram, without a crown (Illus. 2566) [106].

c) KALUGA MASS LEVY.

A sky-blue *banner* with white tracery, gold tassels and edges, and painted depictions: on one side—the Blessed Mother of God of Kaluga, and on the other—the Eminent St Lauretius, Kaluga Miracle Worker, holding in his had a chart on which is written, *"By God's mercy and St. Laurentius's prayers be preserved from the howling hail"* [*"Bozhieyu milostiyu i molitvami Svyatago Lavrentiya ot voyuyushchikh izbavi grad sei"*] (Illus. 2567) [107].

d) ST.-PETERSBURG MASS LEVY.

A white *flag* with a red cross in the center; with a gold inscription on the top and sides of the cross: *"In this sign conquer"* [*"Sim pobedishi"*], and in the corners gold monograms of EMPEROR ALEXANDER I within laurels. Steel spearhead; ribbons and tassels silver, as for regular infantry regiments; white pole (Illus. 2568) [108].

e) NIZHNII-NOVGOROD MASS LEVY.

A white *flag* with gold laurel branches around the edges. On one side is depicted in gold: a cross, crown, monogram of EMPEROR ALEXANDER I, and the inscription: *"For Faith and Tsar"* [*"Za Veru i Tsarya"*]. Along the sides of the cross are the Cyrillic letters N. and O. (*Nizhegorodskoe opolocheni*), and along the sides of the monogram the regimental and battalion numbers. For example, in the 1st Battalion of the 1st Regiment: *1-go P. 1-go B.* On the reverse is shown a dark-red deer with gold antlers, and under it a gold trophy of arms. (*Note: This deer, representing the Nizhni-Novgorod coat of arms, was not entirely accurately displayed on the flags. It should have been red with black antlers and black hoofs.*) The spearheads on the poles were hollow, with the monogram of EMPEROR ALEXANDER I (Illus. 2569) [109].

f) 3RD COMPANY, 2ND BATTALION, 2ND FOOT REGIMENT OF THE KOSTROMA MASS LEVY.

A small yellow flag [*znachek*] on one side of which was painted a gold cross and the monogram of EMPEROR ALEXANDER I, and on the other an unknown coat of arms showing a shield quartered. The upper left of the shield is raspberry with a yellow cross; the upper right and lower left—yellow or gold, without any images, and the lower right—green with a white crescent turned upside down. Above the shield is inscribed in black letters: *"2nd Regiment of the Kostroma mass levy"* [*"Kostromskago opolcheniya 2-go polka"*], and under the shield: *"2nd Battalion 3rd Company"* [*"2-go bataliona 3-i roty"*] (Illus. 2570) [110].

g) 1ST INFANTRY REGIMENT OF THE SIMBIRSK MASS LEVY.

A light-green *flag* with a gold cross in the center and the gold inscription: *"1-go Simbirskago pekhotnago polka"* [*"1st Simbirsk Infantry Regiment's"*]. Black pole with a hollow gilded spearhead in which is the monogram of EMPEROR ALEXANDER I (Illus. 2571a) [111].

h) KHERSON PROVINCIAL LANDOWNER SKARZHINSKII'S SQUADRON.

Small light sky-blue flag with a white border and the image of a white unicorn. Light sky-blue pole with an iron spearhead (Illus. 2571b) [112].

i) PENZA MASS LEVY.

There were 10 flags for the foot *opolchenie* and 4 for the horse. All were of light-green taffeta [*tafta*] with gold galloon trim around the edges and a yellow 1/2-vershok [7/8-inch] wide fringe. All the flags were square and were 1 arshin [28 inches] along the side for infantry and 7 vershoks [12-1/4 inches] for horse. Both kinds had black poles with ahollow gilded spearhead in the center of which was the HIGHEST monogram. For all flags, one side had painted in gold: a monogram, over which was a crown, along the sides of the monogram were laurel wreaths, over the wreaths were the Cyrillic letters P. and O. [for *Poltavskoe opolchenie* –M.C.], and under the wreaths—the designation of the regiment, battalion, or squadron, e.g.: for the 1st Battalion of the 1st Foot Regiment—*1-go polka 1-go bat.* (Illus. 2572a), and for the 3rd Horse Squadron—*Ko. Polka 3-go esk.* (Illus. 2572b). On the other side of the flags was the inscription: *"s nami Bog"* [*"God with us"*], and a gold cross within rays of light. In infantry regiments the cross was similar to the crosses of knightly orders, but straight for horse units. These latter flags also differed from those for infantry in having three gold cords and tassels fastened to the upper part of the pole. In infantry regiments flag poles were 4-1/2 arshins [126 inches] long, and for horse—4 arshins [112 inches] [113].

j) CHERNIGOV MASS LEVY.

1) *1st Battalion of the 1st Regiment*—a white *flag* with gold fringe; in the center a coffee-colored cross with an image of the crucified Saviour. Below the cross the monogram of EMPEROR ALEXANDER I underneath a crown; below the upper edge of the field the inscription *"1-go Chernigovskago polka"* and above the lower edge—*"1-go bataliona."* The monogram and letters, as well as the flag's tassels and cords, were gold; white pole; gilded spearhead with EMPEROR ALEXANDER I's monogram (Illus. 2573a).

2) *The same battalion*—the same *flag* but green, with a green pole (Illus. 2573b).

3) *The 2nd Battalion of the same regiment*—the same *flag* but light sky-blue, with a sky-blue pole (Illus. 2573c).

4) *The 3rd Battalion of the same regiment*—the same *flag* but rose colored, with a red pole (Illus. 2573d).

5) *The 1st Battalion of the 2nd Regiment*—a white *flag* with, in the center, a yellow cross, crown, and monogram, with green wreaths along the sides of these. Under the upper edge of the flag a yellow inscription: *"Slavnyi 1812 god"* [*"The glorious year 1812"*]; below this the yellow Cyrillic letters *Ch.* and *O.*, signifying the *Chernigov opolchenie*, and above the lower edge the yellow inscription: *"Vtorago Chernig. Polka batl. 1-go"* [*"Second Chernigov Regiment's, 1st btn's."*]. The fringe, cords, and tassels were of yellow worsted; yellow pole with a flag iron spearhead on which was engraved EMPEROR ALEXANDER I's monogram under a crown (Illus. 2574a).

6) *The same battalion*—the same *flag* but dark green, with light-gray wreaths (Illus. 2574b).

7) *The 2nd Battalion of the same regiment*—the same *flag* but very dark blue, with light-green wreaths (Illus. 2574c).

8) *The 3rd Battalion of the same regiment*—the same *flag* but dark red, with green wreaths (Illus. 2574d).

9) *The 1st Battalion of the 6th Regiment*—a white *flag* with a painted gold cross, HIGHEST monogram within laurels and under a crown, the letters *Ch.* and *O.*, and the inscription: *"Slavnyi 1812 god, 6-go polka 1-go bataliona."* White pole with the same cords, tassels, and spearhead as in the 1st Regiment (Illus. 2575a).

10) *The 2nd Battalion of the same regiment*—the same *flag* but rose colored, with a sky-blue pole (Illus. 2575b).

11 and 12) *The 3rd Battalion of the same regiment*—the same *flags* but sky blue, with light sky-blue poles, with one flag having the word *"slavnyi"* miswritten as *"slvnyi"* (Illus. 2575c and 2575d).

13) *The Novozybkov Regiment*—a white *flag* with gold fringe and gold inscriptions: below the upper edge—*"Chernigovskoe opolchenie,"* and above the lower edge—*"1812. The Novozybkov Regiment's"*]. In the center the Chernigov coat-of-arms: a black single-headed eagle under a gold crown and with a gold cross in its talons. White pole; spearhead, cords, and tassels as in the preceding flags of the 6th Regiment (Ilus. 2576a).

14) *The Gorodnitsk Regiment*—the same *flag* but green, with the inscription below: *"Gorodnitskago polka,"* and with a dark-green pole (Illus. 2576b) [114].

k) REGIMENTS OF THE POLTAVA MASS LEVY.

A yellow *flag* with gold fringe and gold cross and monogram of EMPEROR ALEXANDER I under a crown and within laurels; with the letters *P.* and *O.* (Poltava *opolchenie*); with an inscription between the cross and monogram: *"Slavnyi 1812 god,"* and the regimental and battalion numbers marked out below, for example: *1-go pol. 2-go bat.* Straw-colored poles; spearhead, cords, and tassels as for the preceding flags (Illus. 2577) [115].

H) MEDALS AND OTHER BADGES ESTABLISHED TO REWARD SERVICE, MARK MILITARY DEEDS, AND COMMEMORATE NOTEWORTHY MILITARY EVENTS, DURING THE REIGN OF EMPEROR ALEXANDER I.

1) In **1804** lower ranks who had taken part in the taking by storm of the Persian fortress of Gandja on 3 January 1804 were given silver *medals* on St.-George ribbon, on the obverse of which was the monogram of EMPEROR ALEXANDER I, and on the reverse of which was the inscription: *"Za trudy i khrabrost' pri vzyatii Ganzhi Genvarya 3 1804 goda"* [*"For service and bravery at the taking of Gandja January 3 1804"*] (Illus. 2578a) [116]. This medal, as all the following medals, was worn in buttonhole of the uniform coat.

2 and 3) **10 October 1806** and **5 February 1807** - because the current military situation could not allow the release of lower ranks from the active force to fill vacancies in provincial companies and state commands, retired lower ranks were invited to enroll in these units. For those who served a term of three years in these companies and commands and then volunteered to remain in service, there was established a silver *medal* inscribed *"Za userdnuyu sluzhbu. 1806"* [*"For zealous service. 1806"*], with a stand of arms on the reverse, and worn on a red ribbon (Illus. 2578b) [117], and for serving a term of six years—the same *medal* but on a sky-blue ribbon, with the inscription: *"V chest' zasluzhennomu soldatu 1806"* [*"In honor of a veteran soldier 1806"*] (Illus. 2578c) [118].

4) **15 March 1807** – with the establishment of the Mobile or Serving Militia, a silver *medal* was instituted for those members who would take part in operational fighting. On the obverse was a bust of EMPEROR ALEXANDER I surrounded by the inscription *"Aleksandr I Imp. Vseross. 1807"* [*"Alexander I Emp. of All the Russ. 1807"*], and on the reverse—the inscription *"Za Veru i Otechestvo. Zemskomu voisku"* [*"For Faith and Fatherland. The Rural Host"*] [119]. With the end of the war with France in that same year of 1807, these medals were distributed to the Mobile Militia in the following manner: gold on

a St.-George ribbon for officers who took part in battles (Illus. 2578d), silver on a St.-George ribbon for militia soldiers who took part in battles (Illus. 2578e), and gold on a St. Vladimir ribbon for officers who had not taken part in any combat (Illus. 2578f) [120].

5) **13 February 1807** – to decorate lower military ranks who while actively serving in army or naval forces "distinguished themselves in the face of the enemy by their outstanding courage," there was established a silver cross on a St.-George ribbon, in the center of which, on the obverse, was an image of St. George on horseback, and on the reverse—the initial letters of the words "St. George," i.e. the Cyrillic letters *S.* and *G.*, one laid over the other. On this same side, on the cross itself, was the serial number marking the seniority of receipt (Illus. 2579a), so that the first cross awarded showed No. 1, the second—No. 2, and so on. This decoration was given the name *Badge of Distinction of the Military Order [Znak otlichiya Voennago Ordena]* [121].

6) **31 August 1807** – to decorate all those officers who had taken part in the battle with the French near the town of Preussisch-Eylau and who had not received orders of St. George or St. Vladimir, but who had been nominated by the Command-in-Chief for a medal, there was established a gold *cross* on a St.-George ribbon, with inscriptions in the center: on the obverse—*"Za trudy i khrabrost'"* ["For deeds and bravery"], and on the reverse—*"Pobeda pri Preish-Eilau 27 Gen. 1807 g."* ["Victory at Preussisch-Eylau 27 Jan. 1807"] (Illus. 2579c) [122].

7 and 8) **14 April 1809** – to commemorate the feats performed by the various corps under the command of Lieutenant General Barclay-de-Tolly and General-Adjutant Graf Shuvalov, as well as the vanguard of Prince Bagration's corps commanded by Major General Kulnev, all of which crossed into Swedish territory: the corps of Baclay-de-Tolly across the part of the Gulf of Bothnia called the Kvarken, the corps of Graf Shuvalov through Torneo, and Kulnev's column—through Alandshaf, there were established silver *medals* for wear by lower ranks on a sky-blue ribbon. On the obverse was the monogram of EMPEROR ALEXANDER I, and on the reverse the inscription—for the troops of Lieutenant General Baclay-de-Tolly and Major General Kulnev—*"Za perekhod na Shvedskii bereg 1809"* ["For the crossing of the Swedish coast 1809"] (Illus. 2579c), and for the troops of Graf Shuvalov—*"Za prokhod v Shvetsiyu chrez Torneo. 1809"* ["For crossing into Sweden through Torneo. 1809"] (Illus. 2579d) [123].

9 and 10) **13 June 1810** – to decorate field and company-grade officers of the corps of Lieutenant General Graf Kamenskii 1 who distinguished themselves at the capture by assault of the Turkish fortress of Bazardzhik, but who did not receive knightly orders, there were instituted gold *crosses* worn on a St.-George ribbon, inscribed on the obverse with *"Za otlichnuyu khrabrost'* ["For distinguished courage"], and on the reverse with *"pri vzyatie pristupom Bazardzhika 2 Maiya 1810 goda"* ["at the taking of Bazardzhik by storm, 22 May 1810"] (Illus. 2580a). Lower ranks who took part in the assault received silver *medals*, also on a St.-George ribbon, on whose face was the bust of EMPEROR ALEXANDER I encircled by the inscription: *"Aleksandr I Imp. Vseross."* ["Alexander I Emp. of All the Russ."]. On the reverse was the inscription *"Za otlichie pri vzyatie pristupom Bazardzhika 22 Maiya 1810 g."* ["For distinction at the taking of Bazardzhik by storm, 22 May 1810"] (Illus. 2580b) [124].

11) **5 February 1813** – to commemorate the Patriotic War of 1812, there was established for all ranks who had taken part a silver *medal* on a sky-blue ribbon. On the face was the All-Seeing Eye within rays of light, under which was written *"1812 god,"* and on the reverse was the inscription *"Ne nam, ne nam, a imeni Tvoemu"* ["Not for us, no us, but in Your name"] (Illus. 2580c) [125].

12) **30 August 1814** – to commemorate the entry of Russian troops into Paris, for all ranks who took part in that event on that day in 1814 it was planned to establish a silver *medal*. It was only distributed during the reign of the SOVEREIGN EMPEROR NICHOLAS PAVLOVICH on 19 March 1826. To be worn on a ribbon that was half sky-blue and half St.-George colors, this medal had on its obverse a bust of EMPEROR ALEXANDER I in a laurel wreath, surrounded by rays of light emanating from the All-Seeing Eye, and on the reverse was the inscription *"Za vzyatie Parizha 19-go Marta 1814"* ["For the taking of Paris 19 March 1814"] (Illus. 2580d) [126].

NOTES

(61) PSZ, Vol. XXIV, pg. 923, No. 22,390.

(62) Moscow Section of the Archive of the War Ministry's Inspection Department, file on Militia, 1806, No. 157/220, bundle I, book "A", and statements by contemporaries.

(63) From the files of the War Ministry's Commissariat Department.

(64) 1) Drawings of the uniforms of the IMPERIAL Militia Battalion, created at the direction of TSESAREVICH CONSTANTINE PAVLOVICH by Academician Orlovskii and given in 1835 by the late GRAND DUKE MICHAEL PAVLOVICH to the Life-Guards Finland Regiment; 2) some actual items preserved up to now; portraits and evidence provided by persons who served in the IMPERIAL Militia Battalion, and 3) *A Short Outline History of the Life-Guards Finland Regiment*, by Major General Marin, who served in the regiment, St. Petersburg 1846, book I, page 10, and book II, pg. 153. The subsequent uniform of the battalion upon its incorporation into the Guards is appropriately located in Volume XIV of *Historical Description of the Clothing and Arms of the Russian Army.*

(65) PSZ, Vol. XXIX, pg. 1039, No. 22,480, and statements by contemporaries.

(66) Ditto.

(67) PSZ, Vol. XXIX, pg. 1047, Nos. 22,498 and 22496, and statements by contemporaries.

(68) Information and a drawing received from the chief of Vladimir Province, in correspondence of 18 Sept. 1847, No. 8856.

(69) Report of the Riga Town Magistrate, 27 May 1847, No. 4354.

(70) PSZ, Vol. XXII, pg. 1114, No. 16,716.

(71) PSZ, Vol. XXX, pg. 456, No. 23,177, and information from the local administration.

(72) Statements by contemporaries who served in the Army of the Dnieper.

(73) Information and drawings received from the Moscow Military Governor-General in correspondence of 11 November 1846, No. 6493, and statements by contemporaries.

(74) The same information.

(75) Information extracted from the files of the Revisions department of the Tver Government Office, 2nd Desk of the recruiting section, regarding the 1812 mass levy, and statements from contemporaries.

(76) Correspondence from the chief of Yaroslavl Province, 21 December 1846, No. 8267.

(77) Information and drawings received from the chief of Vladimir Province in correspondence of 18 Sept. 1847, No. 8856.

(78) Information received from the chief of Ryazan Province in correspondence of 31 May 1847, No. 7477.

(79) Information provided in 1847 to the chief of Tula Province by former members of the Tula mass levy: its commander, Colonel Bobrishchev-Pushkin, Collegial Assessors Khozikov and Speranskii, and retired artillery Lieutenant Novokshchenov. Also, information extracted from the archival files of the Kashira government offices by local police official Makshev-Matonov.

(80) Form the same info.,especially a report from the Kashira police official to the chief of Tula Province, 1 May 1847, No. 352.

(81) Information received in correspondence from the chief of Kaluga Province, 10 February 1847, No. 1777.

(82) Information received from the Vitebsk, Mogilev, and Smolensk governor-general, in correspondence of 8 August 1847, No. 864.

(83) File No. 298 in the archive of the War Ministry's Commissariat Department, "On providing the St.-Petersburg, Novgorod, and other mass levies with pay from the Commissariat, sheets 13 et seq.; Notes regarding the formation and field service itself of the St.-Petersburg mass levy of 1812 and 1813, Naval Captain-Lieutenant B. V. Sht., St. Petersb., 1814; oral statements by persons who served in the St.-Petersburg mass levy, especially the former commander of the 5th *Druzhina*, Senator and Privy Councilor D. M. Mordvinov, and State Councilor R. M. Zotov.

(84) Ditto.

(85) Statements from State Councilor Zotov.

(86) Submission of the Simbirsk Civil Governor to the Committee of Simbirsk military forces, 29 August 1812, No. 4089.

(87) Infor. and drawings received in correspondence form the chief of Nizhnii-Novgorod Province, 6 Nov. 1846, No. 13,463.

(88) Information and drawings received from the chief of Kostroma Province, in correspondence of 4 March 1847, No. 1966.

(89) Information received from the chief of Simbirsk Province, in correspondence of 4 November 1846, No. 8291.

(90) Information and drawings received in 1853 from the Penza Province's Representative of the Nobility, Actual State Councilor Olsufev.

(91) Inforomation provided by the Kazan Military Governor and the chief of Vyatka Province, in correspondence of 4

October 1844, No. 1107, and 22 February 1847, No. 2852, and statements from contemporaries.

(92) Statements from the organizer and former commander of this battalion, Senator and Actual Privy Councilor Prince Obolenskii.

(93) Information and drawings received in correspondence from the chief of Kherson Province, 11 February 1847, No. 2086.

(94) Information and a drawing received from the chief of Chernigov Province in correspondence of 16 July 1847, No. 11,470.

(95) Information provided by the Chernigov, Poltava, and Kharkov governor-general, in correspondence of 4 December 1846, No. 5587, and 23 March 1849, No. 1174.

(96) Information provided by the chief of Vologda Province in correspondence of 23 October 1846, No. 7416, and by persons who served in the St.-Petersburg mass levy.

(97) Information and drawings provided by the chief of Olonets Province in correspondence of 9 August 1847, No. 8885.

(98) Statement by former member of the St.-Petersburg mass levy State Councilor Zotov.

(99) Announcement from the Minister of War, General-of-Infantry Barclay de-Tolly, to the chief of War Ministry departments, Lieutenant General Prince Gorchakov, 16 April 1812, No. 994.

(100) PSZ, Vol. XXXII, pg. 352, No. 25,139.

(101) Plan or proposal for the formation of a corps of Lifland horse and foot jägers, given to it commander, Lieutenant Schmit by the Riga Military Governor, Lieutenant General Essen, 2 August 1812, No. 492.

(102) Report by Courland Civil Governor Sievers to Riga Military Governor Lieutenant General Essen, 22 October 1812, No. 49, and the former's directive from Lieutenant General Essen, 23 October 1812, No. 1030.

(103) PSZ, Vol. XXXII, pg. 501, No. 25,310.

(104) Serveral such flags that came from the Tiraspol Fortress, preserved in the Kiev Arsenal.

(105) The first of these banners is at the Moscow Uspenskii Cathedral and the second at the Preobrazhenskaya Spasskaya Church in that same city. Drawings were provided by the headquarters office of the 4th District of the Ways of Communications.

(106) Drawing of the flag kept at the Ryazan Uspenskii Cathedral, received with correspondence from the chief of Ryazan Province, 31 May 1847, No. 7477.

(107) Drawing of the banner kept at the Kaluga Cathedral, received with correspondence from the chief of Kaluga Province, 10 February 1847, No. 1777.

(108) Flag kept at the old St.-Petersburg arsenal.

(109) Actual flag received with correspondence from the chief of Nizhnii-Novgorod Province, 6 November 1846, No. 13,436.

(110) Drawing of the flag received with correspondence from the chief of Kostroma Province, 4 March 1847, No. 1966.

(111) Drawing of the flag received with correspondence from the chief of Simbirsk Province, 4 November 1846, No. 8291.

(112) Drawing and description of the flag, received with correspondence from the chief of Kherson Province, 14 February 1847, No. 2086.

(113) Information and drawings received in 1853 from the Penza Provincial Representative of the Nobility, Actual State Councilor Olsufev.

(114) Drawings and description of flags preserved in the Chernigov Spasopreobrazhenskii Cathedral, received with correspondence from the chief of Chernigov Province, 16 July 1847, No. 11,470.

(115) Drawing of flags kept at the Poltava Uspenskii Cathedral, received with correspondence from the Chernigov, Poltava, and Kherson Governor-General, 4 December 1846, No. 5587.

(116) This as well as all the following drawings are taken from actual medals and other insignia, and are shown actual size.

(117) PSZ, Vol. XXIX, No. 22,326, pg. 793, article 10, and No. 22,448, pg. 1006, article 3 and 5.

(118). Ditto.

(119) Ibid., Vol. XXIX, No. 22,496, pg. 1051, article 15.

(120) Information extracted from personal service records of members of the Mobile Militia, and testimony from some of these veterans.

(121) PSZ, Vol. XXIX, No. 22,455, pg. 1013.

(122) Ibid., Vol. XXIX, No. 22,606, pg. 1259.

(123) HIGHEST Order, 14 April 1809.

(124) PSZ, Vol. XXXI, No. 24,258, pg. 212.

(125) HIGHEST Order to the forces, 5 February 1813, at Klodawa, and PSZ, Vol. XXXII, No. 25,505, pg. 702.

(126) PSZ, Vol. XXXII, No. 25,761, pg. 907, article 3; HIGHEST Order to the Russian forces, 19 March 1826, and PSZ, 2nd Collection, Vol. I, No. 441, pg. 652.

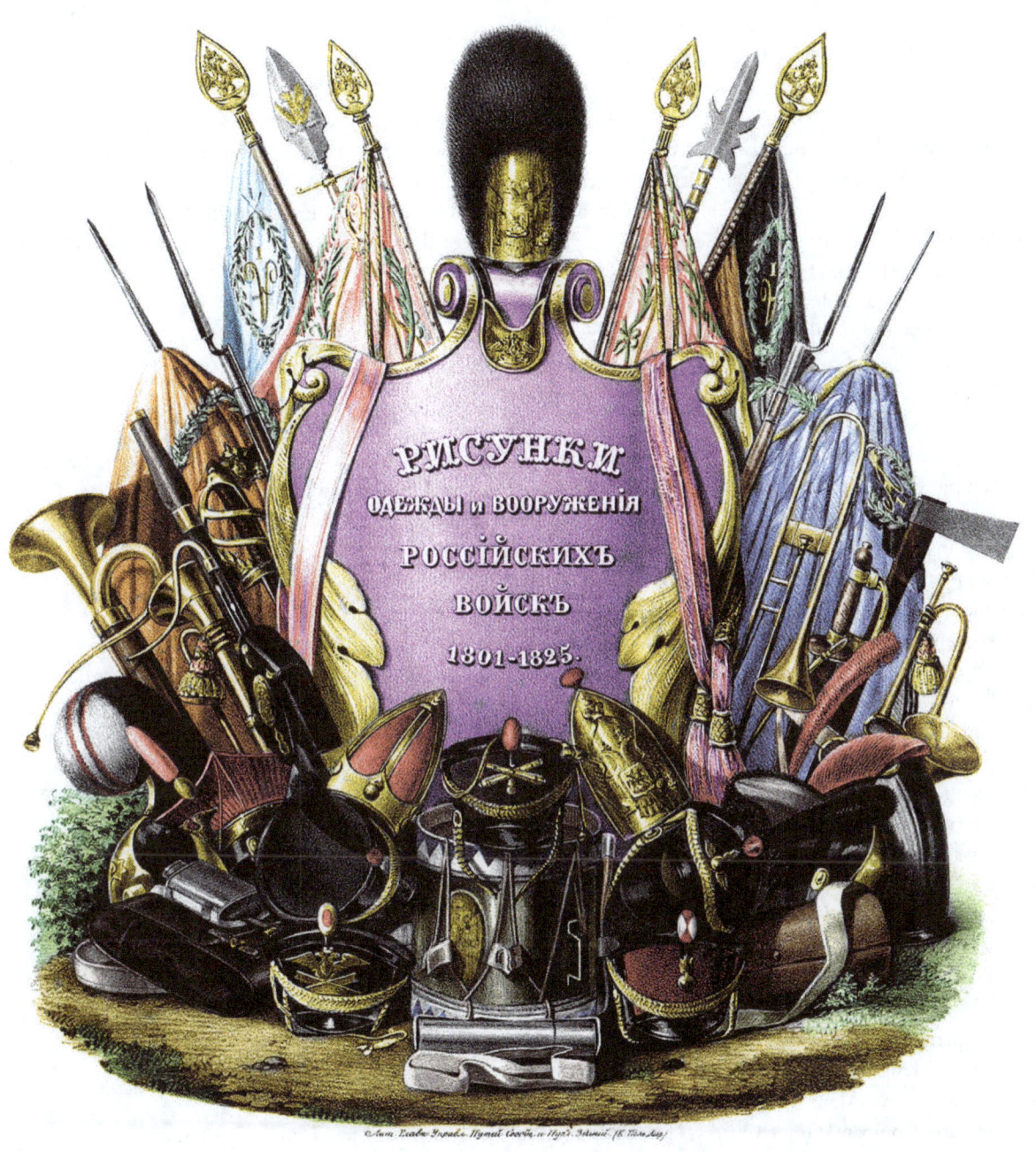

РИСУНКИ
ОДЕЖДЫ и ВООРУЖЕНІЯ
РОССІЙСКИХЪ
ВОЙСКЪ
1801-1825.

PLATES LIST OF ILLUSTRATIONS

2553. Men. Foot Regiments of the Penza Mass Levy, 1812-1813.

2554. Man. Horse Regiment of the Penza Mass Levy, 1812-1813.

2555. Foot and Horse Men. Kazan and Vyatka Mass Levy, 1812-1813.

2556. Private and Company-Grade Off.. HER IMP. HIG. GRAND DUCHESS CATHERINE PAVLOVNA'S Btg, 1812-1814.

2557. Company-Grade Officer and Rear-Rank Cossack. Kherson Landowner Skarzhinskii's Squadron, 1812-1814.

2558. Cossack. Horse Regiments of the Chernigov Mass Levy,, 1812-1815.

2559. Cossack and Non-Commissioned Officer [Unter-Ofitser]. Horse Regiments of the Poltava Mass Levy, 1812-1815.

2560. Company-Grade Officer. Horse Regiments of the Poltava Mass Levy, 1812-1814.

2561. Field-Grade Officer and Cossack. Foot Regiments of the Poltava Mass Levy, 1812-1815.

2562. Marksmen [Strelki]. Mass Levy of Vologda and Olonets Provinces, 1812.

2563. Flag for Mobile Militia battalions, 1807.

2564 and 2565. Banners [Khorugvi] of the Moscow Mass Levy, 1812.

2566. Flag of the 3rd Foot Cossack Regiment of the Ryazan Mass Levy, 1812.

2567. Banner [Khorugv'] of the Kaluga Mass Levy, 1812.

2568. Flag of the St.-Petersburg Mass Levy, 1812.

2569. Flag of the 1st Battalion, 1st Foot Regiment of the Nizhnii-Novgorod Mass Levy, 1812.

2570. Flag [Znachek] of the 3rd Company, 2nd Battalion, 2nd Foot Cossack Regiment of the Kostroma Mass Levy, 1812.

2571. Flag of the 1st Infantry Regiment of the Simbirsk Mass Levy and small flag of Landowner Skarzhinskii's Kherson Squadron, 1812.

2572. Flags of Penza Mass-Levy regiments, 1812. a. Foot regiments. b. Horse regiments.

2573. Flags of the 1st Regiment of the Chernigov Mass Levy, 1812.

2574. Flags of the 2nd Regiment of the Chernigov Mass Levy, 1812.

2575. Flags of the 6th Regiment of the Chernigov Mass Levy, 1812.

2576. Flags of the Novozybkov and Grodnitsk Regiments of the Chernigov Mass Levy, 1812.

2577. Flag of the 2nd Battalion, 1st Regiment of the Poltava Mass Levy, 1812.

2578. Medals instituted from 1804 through 1806: a) for lower ranks who took part in the taking by storm of the fortress of Gandzha, b) for retired lower ranks who served a further three years, c) for those same lower ranks who served a further six years, d) for Officers and e) for men of the Rural Host who took part in battles, f) for Officers of that host who did not take part in battles.

2579. Crosses and Medals instituted from 1807 through 1809: a) lower ranks' Military Order cross for distinction, b) Cross for Officers who distinguished themselves at the Battle of Preussisch-Eylau, c) Medal for lower ranks who took part in the crossing of the Gulf of Bothnia into Sweden, d) Medal for lower ranks who took part in the invasion of Sweden through Torneo.

2580. Crosses and Medals instituted in 1810, 1812, and 1814: a) Cross for Officers and b) Medal for lower ranks who took part in the taking by storm of the fortress of Bazardzhik, c) Medal for Officers and lower ranks commemorating the 1812 war, d) Medal for Officers and lower ranks commemorating the entry into Paris in 1814.

Commander-in-Chief. Region I of the Rural Host, or Militia, 1806-1807.

Provincial Chiefs. Regions II and III of the Rural Host, 1806-1807.

District Chiefs. Regions IV and V of the Rural Host, 1806-1807.

Commanders of a Thousand and Five Hundred. Regions VI and VII of the Rural Host, 1806-1807.

Commander of a Hundred. Region VII of the Rural Hosts, 1806-1807.

Grenadiers. Imperial Militia Battalion, 1806-1808.

Grenadiers. Imperial Militia Battalion, 1806-1808.

Drummer and Non-Commissioned Officer. Grenadier Platoon of the Imperial Militia Battalion, 1806-1808.

Non-Commissioned Officer and Private, Jäger Companies of the Imperial Militia Battalion, 1806-1808.

Gunners [Kanoniry]. Artillery Half-Company of the Imperial Militia Battalion, 1806-1808.

Company-Grade Officers. Grenadier and Jäger Companies of the Imperial Militia Battalion, 1806-1808.

Men [Ratniki]. Rural Host Marksmen Battalions, 1807.

Man [Ratnik]. Mobile or Serving Militia, Vladimir Province, 1807.

Company-Grade Officer. Riga Burgher Company, 1806-1807.

Riga city coat-of-arms.

Foot Cossack and Jäger. Moscow Mass Levy, 1812-1815.

Horse Cossack. Moscow Mass Levy, 1812-1813

2528

Man [Voin] and Company-Grade Officer. Merchants' and Townspeople's Sotnias of the Moscow Mass Levy, 1812–1813.

Company-Grade Officer and Private. Graf Saltykov's Moscow Hussar Regiment, 1812.

Cossack and Company-Grade Officer. Graf Dmitriev-Mamonov's Moscow Cossuckk Regiment, 1812-1814.

Jäger and Foot and Horse Cossacks. Tver Mass Levy, 1812-1813.

Company-Grade Officer and Foot Cossack. Vladimir Mass Levy, 1812-1813.

Foot and Horse Cossacks. Ryazan Mass Levy, 1812-1813

Jäger and Field-Grade Officer, Jäger Regiment of the Tula Mass Levy, 1812-1813.

Company-Grade Officer, Non-Commissioned Officer, and Cossack. Foot Regiments of the Tula Mass Levy, 1812-1813.

Cossack. Horse Regiments of the Tula Muss Levy, 1812.

Field-Grade Officer and General. Horse Regiments of the Tula Mass Levy, 1812-1813.

NCO [Uryadnik] and Mounted Man [Yezdovoi]. Horse Artillery Half-Company of the Tula Mass-Levy, 1812-1814.

Company-Grade Officers. Horse Artillery Half-Company of the Tula Mass Levy, 1812-1813.

Cossack. 1st Horse Cossack Regiment of the Tula Mass Levy, 1813-1814

Men [Voiny]. Foot Bands [Druzhiny] of the St.-Petersburg Mass Levy, 1812-1813.

2542

Non-Commissioned Officer. Foot Bands of the St.-Petersburg Mass Levy, 1812.

Company-Grade Officer. Foot Bands of the St.-Petersburg Mass Levy, 1812

Mon. Foot Bands of the St. Petersburg Mass Levy, 1812 1814.

Field-Grade Officer. Foot Bands of the St.-Petersburg Mass Levy, 1812-1814

Company-Grade Officer of the 2nd and Private of the 3rd Horse Regiments of the St.-Petersburg Mass Levy, 1812-1814.

Foot and Horse Men [Peshii i Konnyi Voiny]. Nizhnii-Novgorod Mass-Levy, 1812-1813.

Foot and Horse Men. Nizhnii-Novgorod Mass-Levy, 1813-1814.

Man and Company-Grade Officer. Horse Regiment of the Kostroma Mass Levy, 1813-1814.

Man. Foot Regiments of the Simbirsk Mass Levy, 1812-1813.

Company-Grade Officer. Foot Regiments of the Simbirsk Mass Levy, 1812-1813.

Man and Field-Grade Officer, Horse Regiment of the Simbirsk Mass Levy, 1813-1814.

Men. Foot Regiments of the Penza Mass Levy, 1812-1813.

Man. Horse Regiment of the Penza Mass Levy, 1812-1813.

Foot and Horse Men. Kazan and Vyatka Mass Levy, 1812-1813.

Private and Company-Grade Off., Her Imp. HIG. GRAND DUCHESS CATHERINE PAVLOVNA'S Btg, 1812-1814

Company-Grade Officer and Rear-Rank Cossack. Kherson Landowner Skarzhinskii's Squadron, 1812-1814.

Cossack. Horse Regiments of the Chernigov Mass Levy,, 1812-1815.

Cossack and Non-Commissioned Officer [Unter-Ofitser]. Horse Regiments of the Poltava Mass Levy, 1812-1815.

Company-Grade Officer. Horse Regiments of the Poltava Mass Levy, 1812-1814.

Field-Grade Officer and Cossack. Foot Regiments of the Poltava Mass Levy, 1812-1815.

Marksmen [Strelki]. Mass Levy of Vologda and Olonets Provinces, 1812.

Flag for Mobile Militia battalions, 1807.

Banners [Khorugvi] of the Moscow Mass Levy, 1812.

2565

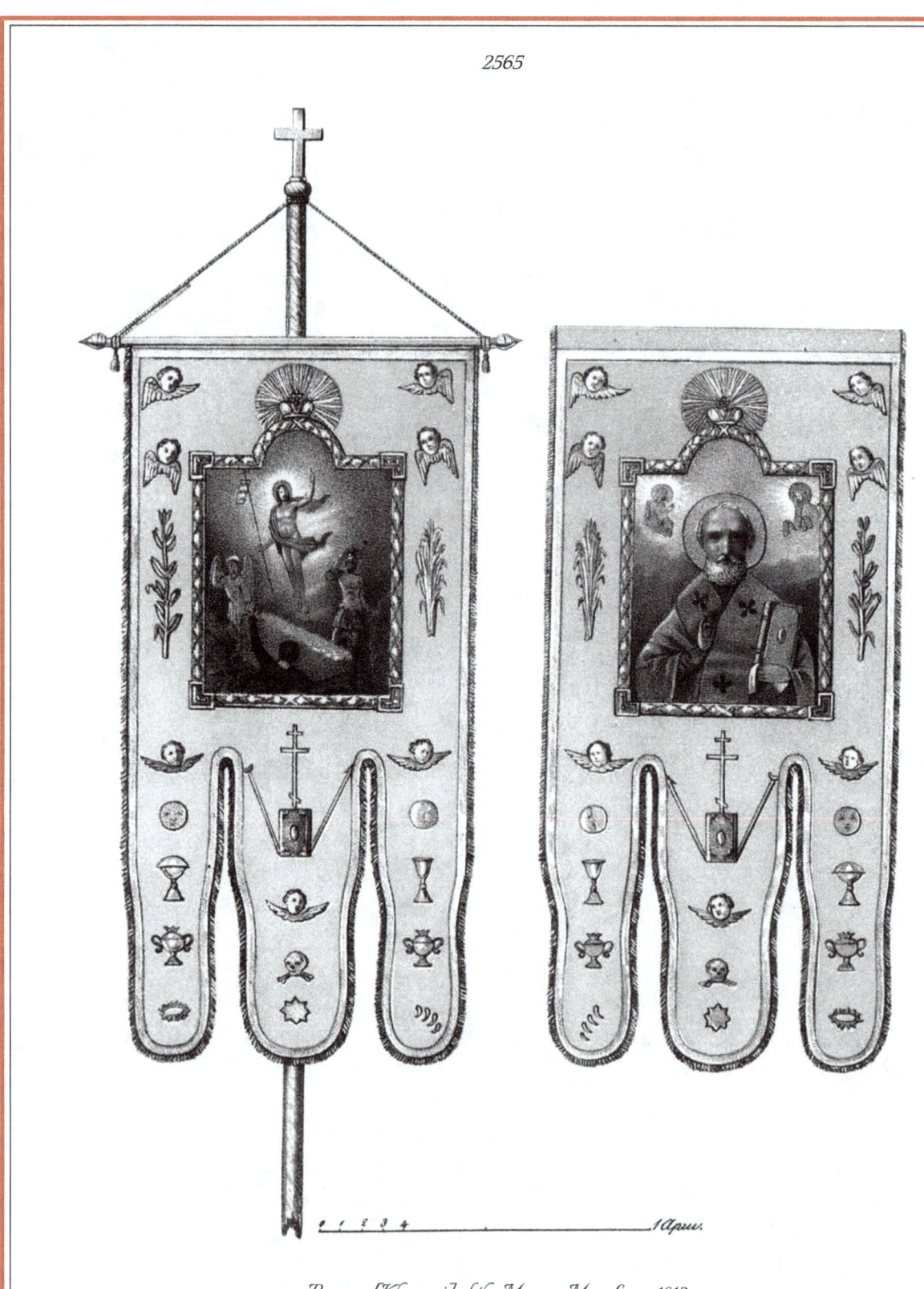

Banners [*Khorugvi*] of the Moscow Mass Levy, 1812.

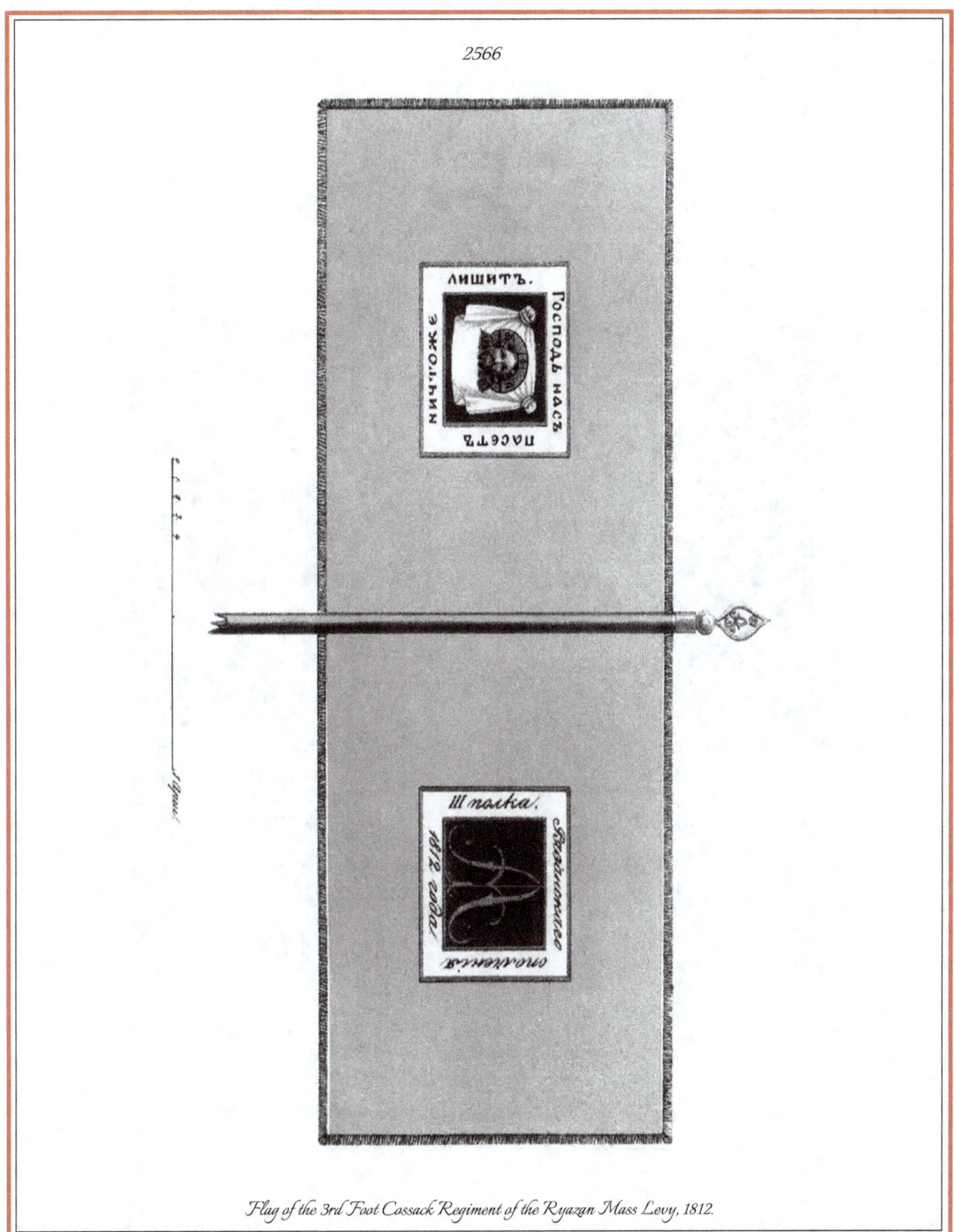

Flag of the 3rd Foot Cossack Regiment of the Ryazan Mass Levy, 1812.

Banner [Khorugv'] of the Kaluga Mass Levy, 1812.

Flag of the St.-Petersburg Mass Levy, 1812

Flag of the 1st Battalion, 1st Foot Regiment of the Nizhnii-Novgorod Mass Levy, 1812.
Flag [Znachek] of the 3rd Company, 2nd Battalion, 2nd Foot Cossack Regiment of the Kostroma Mass Levy, 1812.

a

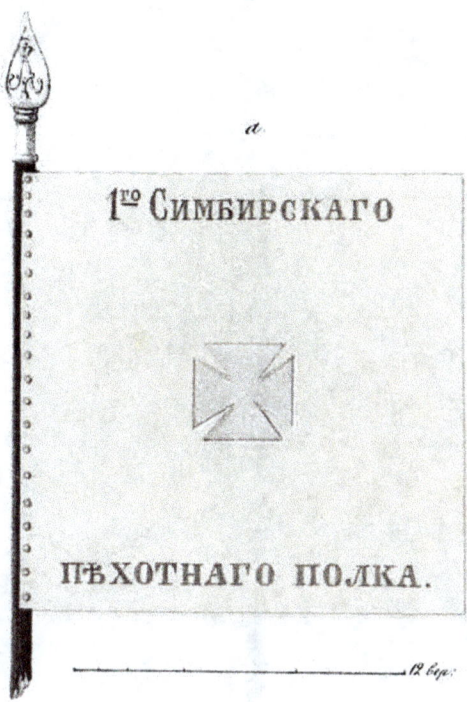

12 вер.

в.

8 вер.

Flag of the 1st Infantry Regiment of the Simbirsk Mass Levy and small flag of Landowner Skarzhinskii's Kherson Squadron, 1812.

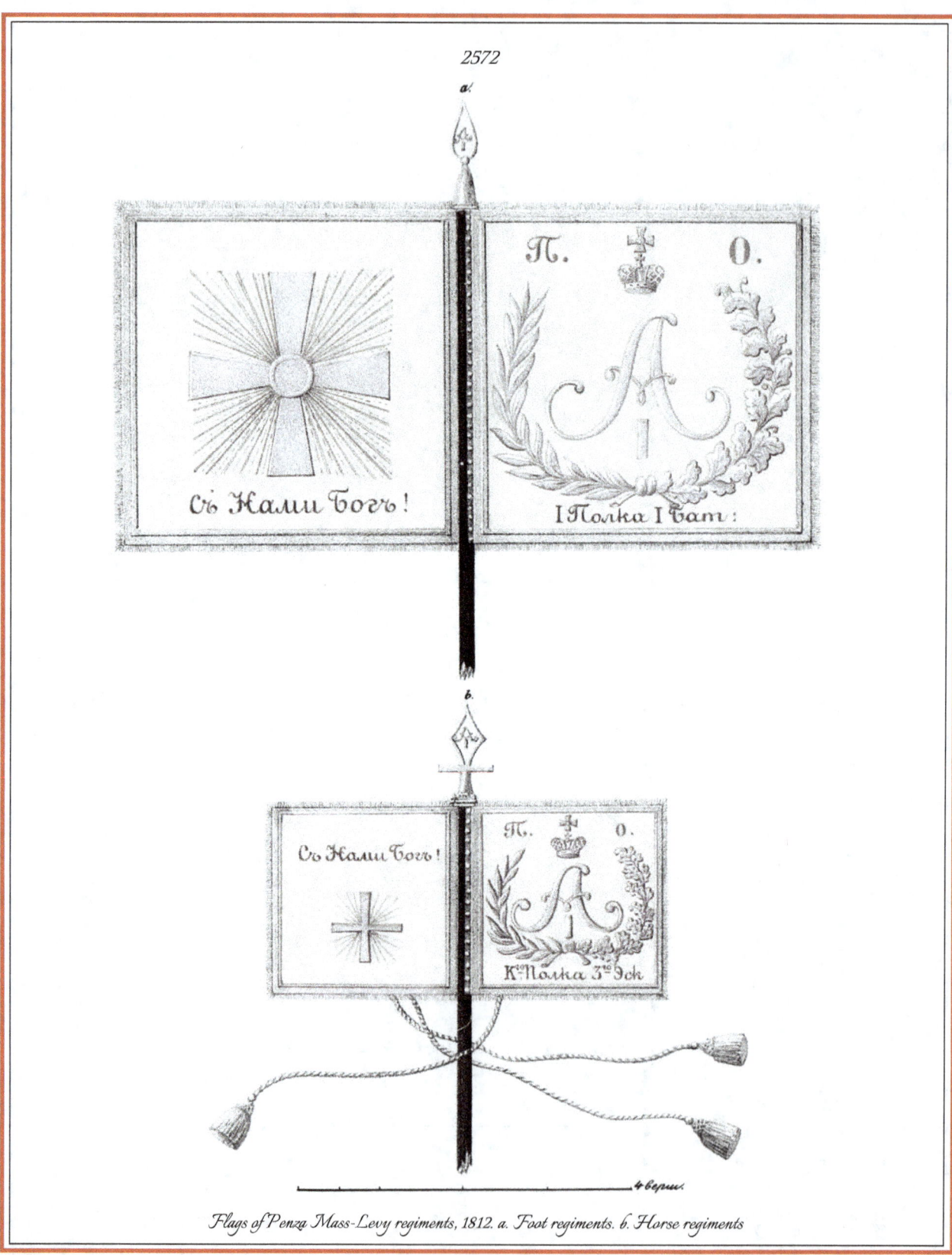

2572

Сь Нами Богъ!

П. О.
I Полка I бат:

Сь Нами Богъ!

П. О.
К. Полка 3го Эск

4 верш.

Flags of Penza Mass-Levy regiments, 1812. a. Foot regiments. b. Horse regiments

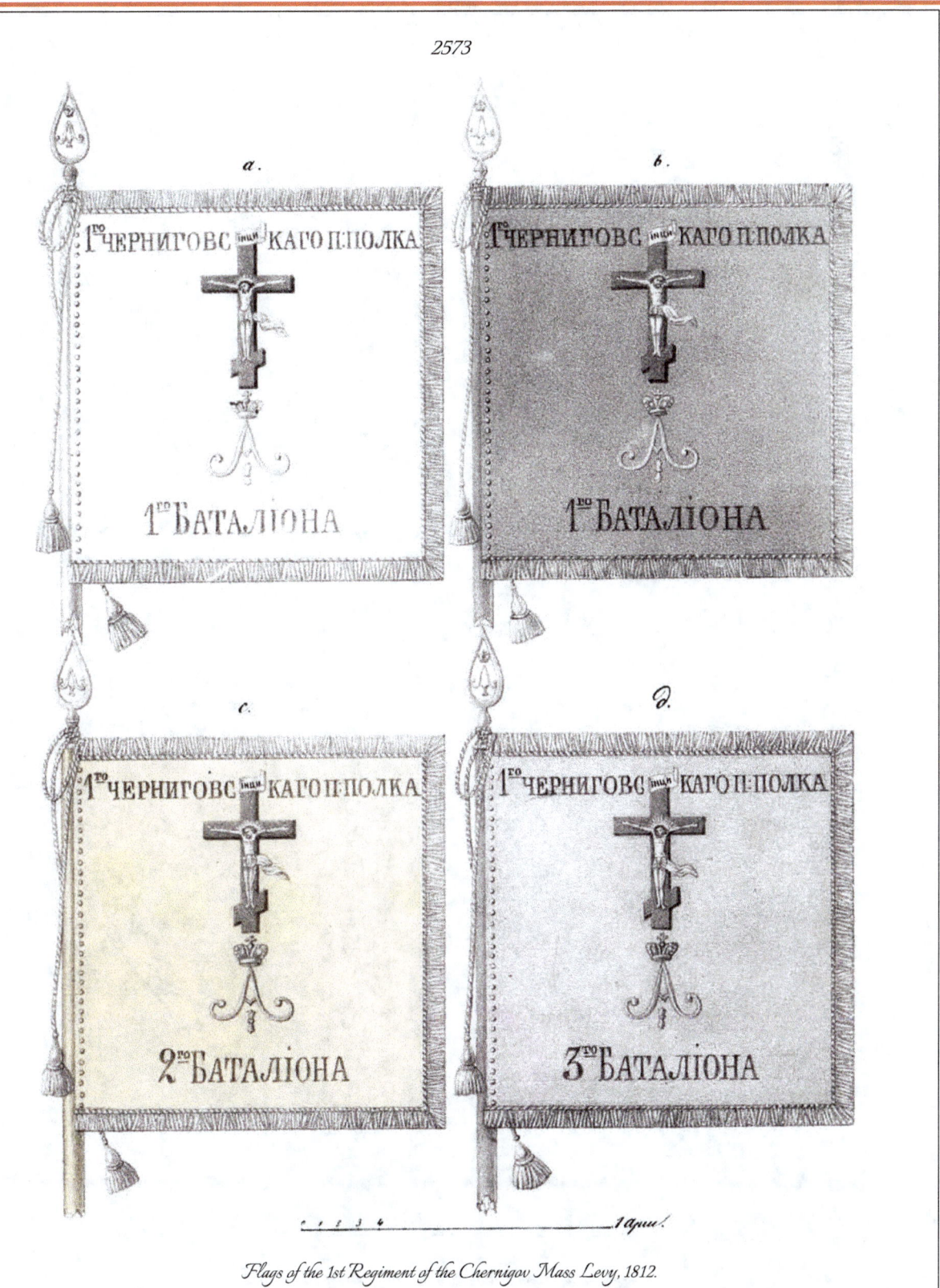

Flags of the 1st Regiment of the Chernigov Mass Levy, 1812.

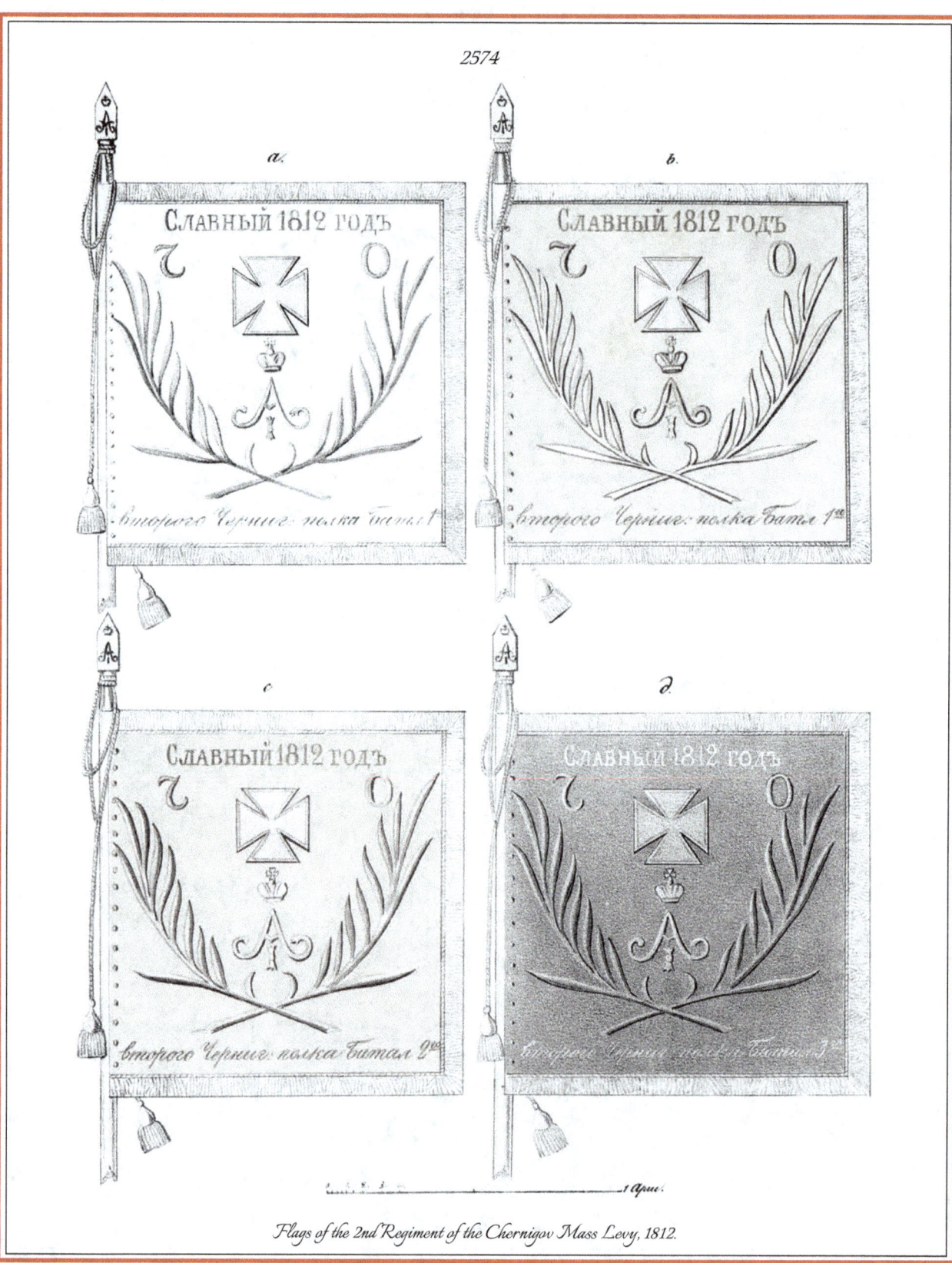

Flags of the 2nd Regiment of the Chernigov Mass Levy, 1812.

Flags of the 6th Regiment of the Chernigov Mass Levy, 1812.

a.

ЧЕРНИГОВСКАГО ОПОЛЧЕНІЯ

1812

НОВОЗЫБКОВСКАГО ПОЛКА

б.

ЧЕРНИГОВСКАГО ОПОЛЧЕНІЯ

1812

ГОРОДНИЦКАГО ПОЛКА

Flags of the Novozybkov and Grodnitsk Regiments of the Chernigov Mass Levy, 1812.

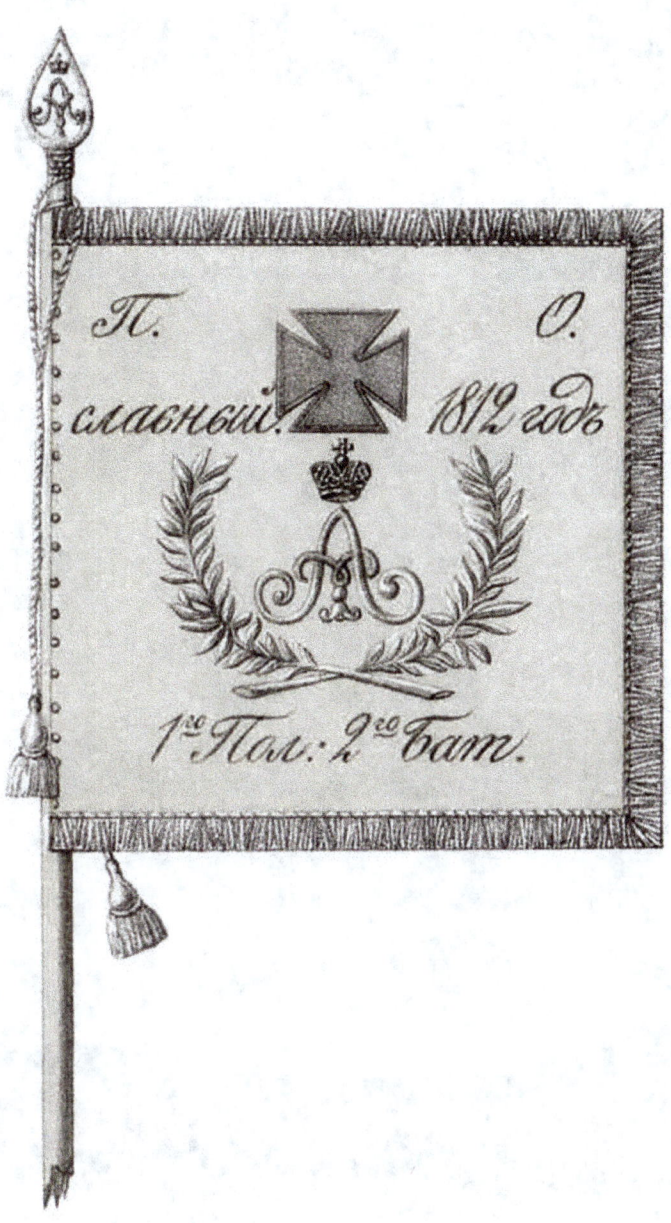

Flag of the 2nd Battalion, 1st Regiment of the Poltava Mass Levy, 1812.

2578

Medals instituted from 1804 through 1806: a) for lower ranks who took part in the taking by storm of the fortress of Gandzha, b) for retired lower ranks who served a further three years, c) for those same lower ranks who served a further six years, d) for Officers and e) for men of the Rural Host who took part in battles, f) for Officers of that host who did not take part in battles.

Crosses and Medals instituted from 1807 through 1809: a) lower ranks' Military Order cross for distinction, b) Cross for Officers who distinguished themselves at the Battle of Preussisch-Eylau, c) Medal for lower ranks who took part in the crossing of the Gulf of Bothnia into Sweden, d) Medal for lower ranks who took part in the invasion of Sweden through Torneo.

Crosses and Medals instituted in 1810, 1812, and 1814: a) Cross for Officers and b) Medal for lower ranks who took part in the taking by storm of the fortress of Bazardzhik, c) Medal for Officers and lower ranks commemorating the 1812 war, d) Medal for Officers and lower ranks commemorating the entry into Paris in 1814.

РАЗБИТІЕ МАРШАЛА ВИКТОРА при Г. СТАРОМЪ БОРИСОВЪ 17-го ноября 1812.

DÉFAITE du MARÉCHAL VICTOR près de la V. de STAROI-BORISSOFF le 17 de novembre 1812.

SOLDIERS, WEAPONS & UNIFORMS ALREADY PUBLISHED
(SOME TITLES)

UNIFORMS OF RUSSIAN ARMY IN THE ERA OF ANCIENT TZAR
FROM THE REIGN OF VASILI IV TO MICHAEL I, ALEXIS, FEODOR III DURING THE XVII th CENTURY
A.V.VISKOVATOV — LUCA STEFANO CRISTINI
SWU-600-004

UNIFORMS OF RUSSIAN ARMY OF PETER I THE GREAT
FROM THE REIGN OF PETER I TO CATHERINE I, PEER II, ANNA AND IVAN VI. 1682-1741
A.V.VISKOVATOV — LUCA STEFANO CRISTINI
SWU-700-006

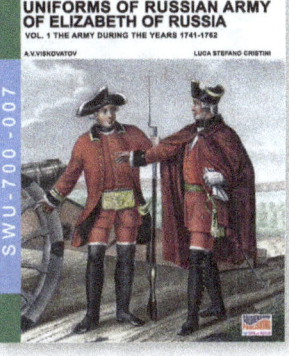

UNIFORMS OF RUSSIAN ARMY OF ELIZABETH OF RUSSIA
VOL. 1 THE ARMY DURING THE YEARS 1741-1762
A.V.VISKOVATOV — LUCA STEFANO CRISTINI
SWU-700-007

UNIFORMS OF RUSSIAN ARMY OF ELIZABETH OF RUSSIA
VOL. 2 THE ARMY DURING THE YEARS 1741-1762
A.V.VISKOVATOV — LUCA STEFANO CRISTINI
SWU-700-008

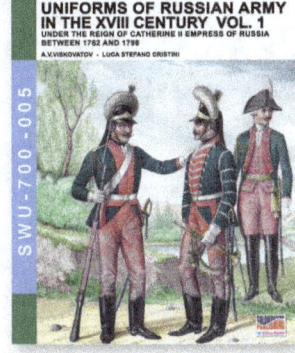

UNIFORMS OF RUSSIAN ARMY IN THE XVIII CENTURY VOL. 1
UNDER THE REIGN OF CATHERINE II EMPRESS OF RUSSIA BETWEEN 1762 AND 1796
A.V.VISKOVATOV — LUCA STEFANO CRISTINI
SWU-700-005

UNIFORMS OF RUSSIAN ARMY IN THE XVIII CENTURY VOL. 2
UNDER THE REIGN OF CATHERINE II EMPRESS OF RUSSIA BETWEEN 1762 AND 1796
A.V.VISKOVATOV — LUCA STEFANO CRISTINI
SWU-700-009

UNIFORMS OF RUSSIAN ARMY IN THE XVIII CENTURY VOL. 3
UNDER THE REIGN OF CATHERINE II EMPRESS OF RUSSIA BETWEEN 1762 AND 1796
A.V.VISKOVATOV — LUCA STEFANO CRISTINI
SWU-700-010

UNIFORMS OF RUSSIAN ARMY IN THE XVIII CENTURY VOL. 4
UNDER THE REIGN OF CATHERINE II EMPRESS OF RUSSIA BETWEEN 1762 AND 1796
A.V.VISKOVATOV — LUCA STEFANO CRISTINI
SWU-700-011

BRITISH ARMY UNIFORMS IN 1742
IN THE ART OF JOHN PINE
SWU-700-001

PRUSSIAN & AUSTRIAN ARMY UNIFORMS IN 1742-1770
LUCA STEFANO CRISTINI
SWU-700-002

THE FRENCH ARMY OF ANCIEN RÉGIME Volume 1
IN THE ART OF FELIX PHILIPPOTEAUX
LUCA STEFANO CRISTINI
SWU-700-003

THE FRENCH ARMY OF ANCIEN RÉGIME Volume 2
IN THE ART OF FELIX PHILIPPOTEAUX
LUCA STEFANO CRISTINI
SWU-700-004

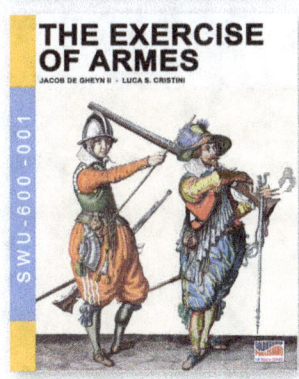

THE EXERCISE OF ARMES
JACOB DE GHEYN II — LUCA S. CRISTINI
SWU-600-001

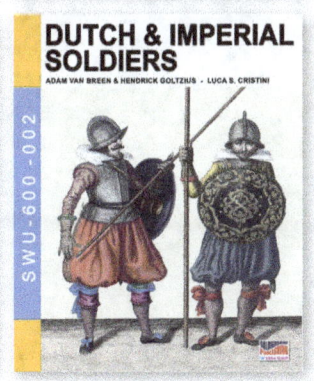

DUTCH & IMPERIAL SOLDIERS
ADAM VAN BREEN & HENDRICK GOLTZIUS — LUCA S. CRISTINI
SWU-600-002

HORSEMEN IN THE 16TH & 17TH C.
JACOB DE GHEYN II — A.DE BRUYN — LUCA S. CRISTINI
SWU-600-003

IMPERIAL SOLDIERS & UNIFORMS 1640-1860
IN THE ART OF FRANZ GERASCH
LUCA S.CRISTINI   Plates by FRANZ GERASCH
SWU-GEN-001